DAVID FOSTER WALLACE

DAVID FOSTER WALLACE
THE LAST INTERVIEW
and OTHER CONVERSATIONS

MELVILLE HOUSE
BROOKLYN · LONDON

DAVID FOSTER WALLACE: THE LAST INTERVIEW

© 2012 Melville House Publishing

"There Can Be No Spokesman" © Tom Scocca. Interview conducted for the *Boston Phoenix*, which published an edited version in 1998.

A Brief Interview with a Five-Draft Man: First published in *Amherst* magazine, published by the Trustees of Amherst College.

"To Try Extra Hard to Exercise Patience, Politeness, and Imagination": This interview first appeared in the November 2003 issue of the *Believer*. Reprinted by permission.

"Some Kind of Terrible Burden": first broadcast on "To the Best of Our Knowledge," a production of Wisconsin Public Radio and Steve Paulson, Executive Producer. © 2004 Board of Regents of the University of Wisconsin System.

The Last Interview: Reprinted by permission of the *Wall Street Journal*, © 2008 Dow Jones & Company, Inc. All Rights Reserved Worldwide. License number 2938361379117

First Melville House printing: December 2012

Melville House Publishing
145 Plymouth Street
Brooklyn, NY 11201

www.mhpbooks.com

ISBN: 978-1-61219-206-2
1 2 3 4 5 6 7 8 9 10

Manufactured in the United States of America

A catalog record for this book is available from the Library of Congress

CONTENTS

"SOMETHING REAL AMERICAN"

INTERVIEW BY LAURA MILLER

FIRST PUBLISHED IN *SALON*

MARCH 9, 1996

David Foster Wallace's low-key, bookish appearance flatly contradicts the unshaven, bandanna-capped image advanced by his publicity photos. But then, even a hipster novelist would have to be a serious, disciplined writer to produce a 1,079-page book in three years. *Infinite Jest*, Wallace's mammoth second novel, juxtaposes life in an elite tennis academy with the struggles of the residents of a nearby halfway house, all against a near-future background in which the US, Canada and Mexico have merged, Northern New England has become a vast toxic waste dump and everything from private automobiles to the very years themselves are sponsored by corporate advertisers. Slangy, ambitious and occasionally over-enamored with the prodigious intellect of its author, *Infinite Jest* nevertheless has enough solid emotional ballast to keep it from capsizing. And there's something rare and exhilarating about a contemporary author who aims to capture the spirit of his age.

The 34-year-old Wallace, who teaches at Illinois State University in Bloomington-Normal and exhibits the careful modesty of a recovering smart aleck, discussed American life on the verge of the millennium, the pervasive influence of pop culture, the role of fiction writers in an entertainment-saturated society, teaching literature to freshmen and his own maddening, inspired creation during a recent reading tour for *Infinite Jest*.

MILLER: What were you intending to do when you started this book?

DFW: I wanted to do something sad. I'd done some funny stuff and some heavy, intellectual stuff, but I'd never done anything sad. And I wanted it not to have a single main character. The other banality would be: I wanted to do something real American, about what it's like to live in America around the millennium.

MILLER: And what is that like?

DFW: There's something particularly sad about it, something that doesn't have very much to do with physical circumstances, or the economy, or any of the stuff that gets talked about in the news. It's more like a stomach-level sadness. I see it in myself and my friends in different ways. It manifests itself as a kind of lostness. Whether it's unique to our generation I really don't know.

MILLER: Not much of the press about *Infinite Jest* addresses the role that Alcoholics Anonymous plays in the story. How does that connect with your overall theme?

DFW: The sadness that the book is about, and that I was going through, was a real American type of sadness. I was white, upper-middle-class, obscenely well-educated, had had way more career success than I could have legitimately hoped for and was sort of adrift. A lot of my friends were the same way. Some of them were deeply into drugs, others were unbelievable workaholics. Some were going to singles bars every night. You could see it played out in 20 different ways, but it's the same thing.

Some of my friends got into AA. I didn't start out wanting to write a lot of AA stuff, but I knew I wanted to do drug addicts and I knew I wanted to have a halfway house. I went to a couple of meetings with these guys and thought that it was tremendously powerful. That part of the book is supposed to be living enough to be realistic, but it's also supposed to stand for a response to lostness and what you do when the things you thought were going to make you OK, don't. The bottoming out with drugs and the AA response to that was the starkest thing that I could find to talk about that.

I get the feeling that a lot of us, privileged Americans, as we enter our early 30s, have to find a way to put away childish things and confront stuff about spirituality and values. Probably the AA model isn't the only way to do it, but it seems to me to be one of the more vigorous.

MILLER: The characters have to struggle with the fact that the AA system is teaching them fairly deep things through these seemingly simplistic clichés.

DFW: It's hard for the ones with some education, which,

to be mercenary, is who this book is targeted at. I mean this is caviar for the general literary fiction reader. For me there was a real repulsion at the beginning. "One Day at a Time," right? I'm thinking 1977, Norman Lear, starring Bonnie Franklin. Show me the needlepointed sampler this is written on. But apparently part of addiction is that you need the substance so bad that when they take it away from you, you want to die. And it's so awful that the only way to deal with it is to build a wall at midnight and not look over it. Something as banal and reductive as "One Day at a Time" enabled these people to walk through hell, which from what I could see the first six months of detox is. That struck me.

It seems to me that the intellectualization and aestheticizing of principles and values in this country is one of the things that's gutted our generation. All the things that my parents said to me, like "It's really important not to lie." OK, check, got it. I nod at that but I really don't feel it. Until I get to be about 30 and I realize that if I lie to you, I also can't trust you. I feel that I'm in pain, I'm nervous, I'm lonely and I can't figure out why. Then I realize, "Oh, perhaps the way to deal with this is really not to lie." The idea that something so simple and, really, so aesthetically uninteresting—which for me meant you pass over it for the interesting, complex stuff—can actually be nourishing in a way that arch, meta, ironic, pomo stuff can't, that seems to me to be important. That seems to me like something our generation needs to feel.

MILLER: Are you trying to find similar meanings in the pop culture material you use? That sort of thing can be seen as merely clever, or shallow.

DFW: I've always thought of myself as a realist. I can remember fighting with my professors about it in grad school. The world that I live in consists of 250 advertisements a day and any number of unbelievably entertaining options, most of which are subsidized by corporations that want to sell me things. The whole way that the world acts on my nerve endings is bound up with stuff that the guys with leather patches on their elbows would consider pop or trivial or ephemeral. I use a fair amount of pop stuff in my fiction, but what I mean by it is nothing different than what other people mean in writing about trees and parks and having to walk to the river to get water a 100 years ago. It's just the texture of the world I live in.

MILLER: What's it like to be a young fiction writer today, in terms of getting started, building a career and so on?

DFW: Personally, I think it's a really neat time. I've got friends who disagree. Literary fiction and poetry are real marginalized right now. There's a fallacy that some of my friends sometimes fall into, the ol' "The audience is stupid. The audience only wants to go this deep. Poor us, we're marginalized because of TV, the great hypnotic blah, blah." You can sit around and have these pity parties for yourself. Of course this is bullshit. If an art form is marginalized it's because it's not speaking to people. One possible reason is that the people it's speaking to have become too stupid to appreciate it. That seems a little easy to me.

If you, the writer, succumb to the idea that the audience is too stupid, then there are two pitfalls. Number one is the avant-garde pitfall, where you have the idea that you're writing for other writers, so you don't worry about making yourself accessible or relevant. You worry about making it structurally and technically cutting edge: involuted in the right ways, making the appropriate intertextual references, making it look smart. Not really caring about whether you're communicating with a reader who cares something about that feeling in the stomach which is why we read. Then, the other end of it is very crass, cynical, commercial pieces of fiction that are done in a formulaic way—essentially television on the page—that manipulate the reader, that set out grotesquely simplified stuff in a childishly riveting way.

What's weird is that I see these two sides fight with each other and really they both come out of the same thing, which is a contempt for the reader, an idea that literature's current marginalization is the reader's fault. The project that's worth trying is to do stuff that has some of the richness and challenge and emotional and intellectual difficulty of avant-garde literary stuff, stuff that makes the reader confront things rather than ignore them, but to do that in such a way that it's also pleasurable to read. The reader feels like someone is talking to him rather than striking a number of poses.

Part of it has to do with living in an era when there's so much entertainment available, genuine entertainment, and figuring out how fiction is going to stake out its territory in that sort of era. You can try to confront what it is that makes fiction magical in a way that other kinds of art and entertainment aren't. And to figure out how fiction can engage a reader, much of whose sensibility has been formed by pop culture, without simply becoming more shit in the pop culture machine. It's unbelievably difficult and confusing and scary, but it's neat.

There's so much mass commercial entertainment that's so good and so slick, this is something that I don't think any other generation has confronted. That's what it's like to be a writer now. I think it's the best time to be alive ever and it's probably the best time to be a writer. I'm not sure it's the easiest time.

MILLER: What do you think is uniquely magical about fiction?

DFW: Oh, Lordy, that could take a whole day! Well, the first line of attack for that question is that there is this existential loneliness in the real world. I don't know what you're thinking or what it's like inside you and you don't know what it's like inside me. In fiction I think we can leap over that wall itself in a certain way. But that's just the first level, because the idea of mental or emotional intimacy with a character is a delusion or a contrivance that's set up through art by the writer. There's another level that a piece of fiction is a conversation. There's a relationship set up between the reader and the writer that's very strange and very complicated and hard to talk about. A really great piece of fiction for me may or may not take me away and make me forget that I'm sitting in a chair. There's real commercial stuff can do that, and a riveting plot can do that, but it doesn't make me feel less lonely.

There's a kind of Ah-ha! Somebody at least for a moment feels about something or sees something the way that I do. It doesn't happen all the time. It's these brief flashes or flames, but I get that sometimes. I feel unalone—intellectually, emotionally, spiritually. I feel human and unalone and that I'm in a deep, significant conversation with another consciousness in fiction and poetry in a way that I don't with other art.

MILLER: Who are the writers who do this for you?

DFW: Here's the hard thing about talking about that: I don't mean to say my work is as good as theirs. I'm talking about stars you steer by.

MILLER: Understood.

DFW: OK. Historically the stuff that's sort of rung my cherries: Socrates' funeral oration, the poetry of John Donne, the poetry of Richard Crashaw, every once in a while Shakespeare, although not all that often, Keats' shorter stuff, Schopenhauer, Descartes' *Meditations on First Philosophy* and *Discourse on Method*, Kant's *Prolegomena to Any*

Future Metaphysic, although the translations are all terrible, William James' *Varieties of Religious Experience*, Wittgenstein's *Tractatus*, Joyce's *Portrait of the Artist as a Young Man*, Hemingway—particularly the ital stuff in *In Our Time*, where you just go oomph!, Flannery O'Connor, Cormac McCarthy, Don DeLillo, A.S. Byatt, Cynthia Ozick—the stories, especially one called 'Levitations,' about 25 percent of the time Pynchon. Donald Barthelme, especially a story called 'The Balloon,' which is the first story I ever read that made me want to be a writer, Tobias Wolff, Raymond Carver's best stuff—the really famous stuff. Steinbeck when he's not beating his drum, 35 percent of Stephen Crane, *Moby-Dick*, *The Great Gatsby*.

And, my God, there's poetry. Probably Phillip Larkin more than anyone else, Louise Glück, Auden.

MILLER: What about colleagues?

DFW: There's the whole "great white male" deal. I think there are about five of us under 40 who are white and over 6 feet and wear glasses. There's Richard Powers who lives only about 45 minutes away from me and who I've met all of once. William Vollmann, Jonathan Franzen, Donald Antrim, Jeffrey Eugenides, Rick Moody. The person I'm highest on right now is George Saunders, whose book *Civilwarland in Bad Decline* just came out, and is well worth a great deal of attention. A.M. Homes: her longer stuff I don't think is perfect, but every few pages there's something that just doubles you over. Kathryn Harrison, Mary Karr, who's best known for *The Liars' Club* but is also a poet and I think the best female poet under 50. A woman named Cris Mazza. Rikki Ducornet, Carole Maso. Carole Maso's *Ava* is just—a friend of mine read it and said it gave him an erection of the heart.

MILLER: Tell me about your teaching.

DFW: I was hired to teach creative writing, which I don't like to teach.

There's two weeks of stuff you can teach someone who hasn't written 50 things yet and is still kind of learning. Then it becomes more a matter of managing various people's subjective impressions about how to tell the truth vs. obliterating someone's ego.

I like to teach freshman lit because ISB gets a lot of rural students who aren't very well educated and don't like to read. They've grown up thinking that literature means dry, irrelevant, unfun stuff, like cod liver oil. Getting to show them some more contemporary stuff—the one we always do the second week is a story called 'A Real Doll,' by A.M. Homes, from *The Safety of Objects*, about a boy's affair with a Barbie doll. It's very smart, but on the surface, it's very twisted and sick and riveting and real relevant to people who are 18 and five or six years ago were either playing with dolls or being sadistic to their sisters. To watch these kids realize that reading literary stuff is sometimes hard work, but it's sometimes worth it and that reading literary stuff can give you things that you can't get otherwise, to see them wake up to that is extremely cool.

MILLER: How do you feel about the reaction to the length of your book? Did it just sort of wind up being that long, or do you feel that you're aiming for a particular effect or statement?

DFW: I know it's risky because it's part of this equation of making demands on the reader—which start out financial. The other side of it is publishing houses hate it because they make less money. Paper is so expensive. If the length seems gratuitous, as it did to a very charming Japanese lady from the *New York Times*, then one arouses ire. And I'm aware of that. The manuscript that I delivered was 1700 manuscript pages, of which close to 500 were cut. So this editor didn't just buy the book and shepherd it. He line-edited it twice. I flew to New York, and all that. If it looks chaotic, good, but everything that's in there is in there on purpose. I'm in a good emotional position to take shit for the length because if the length strikes people as gratuitous, then the book just fails. It's not gratuitous because I didn't feel like working on it or making the cuts.

It's a weird book. It doesn't move the way normal books do. It's got a whole bunch of characters. I think it makes at least an in-good-faith attempt to be fun and riveting enough on a page-by-page level so I don't feel like I'm hitting the reader with a mallet, you know, "Hey, here's this really hard impossibly smart thing. Fuck you. See if you can read it." I know books like that and they piss me off.

MILLER: What made you choose a tennis academy, which mirrors the halfway house in the book?

DFW: I wanted to do something with sport and the idea of dedication to a pursuit being kind of like an addiction.

MILLER: Some of the characters wonder if it's worth it, the competitive obsession.

DFW: It's probably like this in anything. I see my students do this with me. You're a young writer. You admire an older writer, and you want to get to where that older writer is. You imagine that all the energy that your envy is putting into it has somehow been transferred to him, that there's a flipside to it, a feeling of being envied that's a good feeling the way that envy is a hard feeling. You can see it as the idea of being in things for some kind of imaginary goal involving prestige rather than for the pursuit itself. It's a very American illness, the idea of giving yourself away entirely to the idea of working in order to achieve some sort of brass ring that usually involves people feeling some way about you—I mean, people wonder why we walk around feeling alienated and lonely and stressed out?

Tennis is the one sport I know enough about for it to be beautiful to me, for me to think that it means something. The nice thing about it is that I've got *Tennis* magazine wanting to do something about me. For me personally it's been great. I may get to hit with the pros some day. It has that advantage.

"THERE CAN BE NO SPOKESMAN"

INTERVIEW BY TOM SCOCCA

EDITED VERSION FIRST PUBLISHED
IN THE *BOSTON PHOENIX*

FEBRUARY 20, 1998

Q: For basic reader orientation here, are you doing this from Bloomington?

DFW: Speaking to you? Yes, sir.

Q: What sort of phone?

DFW: What sort of phone? What kind of phone is this? This is a Panasonic Easa-Phone. E-A-S-A, hyphen, P-H-O-N-E. And I don't see a model number on it. It's got a little answering machine attached, although the answering machine doesn't work as often as the average consumer probably would like it to.

Q: OK. Let's see.

DFW: You're really going to orient that reader, aren't you?

Q: Yeah. You have to bring the color in somehow.

DFW: Uh-huh.

Q: Any particular configuration of beard or bandana or glasses? It seems to change over time.

DFW: So what, we're going to pretend, we're going to pretend that we're sitting in the same room?

Q: No.

DFW: I've never had a beard. I've tried periodically to grow a beard, and when it resembles, you know, the armpit of a 15-year-old girl who hasn't shaved her armpit, I shave it off. I do not have a head hanky on at this point, although I did recently, 'cause I just got back from running my dogs around the countryside.

Q: OK. How many dogs?

DFW: This is what's technically known as "soft news," isn't it?

Q: Yes. So how many dogs?

DFW: I have two dogs, who need a great deal of exercise to keep damage from being done to the house.

Q: Are they border collies or something?

DFW: They are—well, they're both mutts, but they're mostly black Lab, but they're large and prone to mischief. They need to be tired out daily or else they chew the walls. Which has a deleterious effect on property values, I'm told.

Q: Are you looking forward to seeing Boston?

DFW: Yeah, I was there, when was I there? I was there two years ago, to—no, I was there last year, actually, and I read at the Brattle Theater. I think that was last year. And I just got back, actually, last night, went and saw *Good Will Hunting*. Which takes place not exactly where I used to live in Boston, but pretty darn close, and so I've been all flush with nostalgia.

Q: As far as you can tell, is the nonfiction work attracting different readers, or is it getting a different sort of reaction than the fiction has?

DFW: Boy, that's a good question. I think people are somewhat less interested in nonfiction, so I think there's been rather less fuss about this book. These were also pieces that were done over six or seven years and then got rewritten right at the end, but, you know, I don't really have much of an emotional investment in them. So it's kind of, it's a more relaxed book, at least for me. In terms of readership, I really have no idea. I stay very far away from that stuff.

Q: How do the different kinds of writing differ for you, fiction versus nonfiction?

DFW: Oh, Lord. Is this an aesthetic question, a process question?

Q: Aesthetic, process, intellectual.

DFW: Golly. You know, the weird thing about the nonfiction is, I don't really think, I mean, I'm not a journalist, and I don't pretend to be one, and most of the pieces in there were assigned to me by *Harper's*, with these sort of maddening instructions of, you know, just go to a certain spot and kind of, you know, turn 350 degrees a few times and tell us what you see.

And so there's a kind of vagueness about the assignment and a kind of, it's more—I'm not being very articulate. I'll be honest. I think of myself as a fiction writer. I'm real interested in fiction, and all elements of fiction. Fiction's more important to me. So I'm also I think more scared and tense about fiction, more worried about my stuff, more worried about whether I'm any good or not, or I'm on the wrong track or not.

Whereas the thing that was fun about a lot of the nonfiction is, you know, it's not that I didn't care, but it was just mostly like, yeah, I'll try this. I'm not an expert at it. I don't pretend to be. It's not particularly important to me whether the magazine, you know, even takes the thing I do or not. And so it was just more, I guess the nonfiction seems a lot more like play. For me.

The weird thing is that when a couple of the nonfiction pieces got attention and then other magazines started to call, then of course I start thinking of myself as doing that, too, and begin—Mr. Ego gets in there, and then I begin worrying and sweating over that stuff, too, so.

Does that sound anything like an answer to the question?

Q: Yeah, that is something like an answer to the question. You cover a pretty wide range of stuff, given the number of essays. As you're getting more offers, are there things that you don't want to write about?

DFW: Well, I've decided I'm not going to do any more of that stuff for a while, just 'cause I'll use it as an excuse not to work on fiction. So. Yeah, there was a lot—I mean, the funny thing is, is I think magazines—there's so much competition with magazines, and I think they're all so desperate for stuff that like, when was it? Actually there was that really long one about the cruise, and a version of it appeared in *Harper's*, and some of the editors liked it, and for I think about like six days, I was really hot. You know, with these editors.

And so there would be these offers, like, I'm trying to remember what some of them were. Well, I won't tell you the names of the magazines, but there was one offer to go to a nudist colony and write about going to a nudist colony. There was one offer to go to, Elizabeth Taylor was having like the product launch of some new brand of perfume, which bizarrely was being held at an Air Force base. And there was an offer to interview David Bowie. What about, I really don't know. I don't know anything about David Bowie.

But so, the weird thing is, for a while there were all

these offers, and it was really neat, 'cause I just, I got to take—I took a couple that I thought were going to be kind of interesting to me, or that I might have anything to write about, but most of them, I just kind of laughed and said, thanks, anyway.

So I think the answer to the question is, the wide range represents the fact that those were just certain times when magazines would call up and say, "Do you want to do X?" and "Do you want to do Y?" and I would go do it. It wasn't really like I sat down and said, OK, I want to do two essays about this and four about that.

Q: Did *Tennis* magazine come to you for the stuff you've written for them?

DFW: Yeah, except I don't think—originally, I did one piece on the US Open for *Tennis* and one piece on that pro guy for *Esquire*. No, the one in *Tennis* isn't in.

Q: Right.

DFW: Because the editor of the book decided he didn't want two. But no, yes, *Tennis* magazine came to me and it was like a serious thrill, because I had of course as a child read *Tennis* magazine and tried out their little drill instructions with masking tape on the local courts and stuff. And so when the big call came, I was of course right there clicking my heels together, ready to go to the US Open.

Q: And how do the editors at *Tennis* react to getting a piece of your style of prose?

DFW: I don't think they had any problem with it. But my big problem with magazines is that I tend, um, they tend to have word lengths. That I try really hard to hew to and then sort of get into it and exceed. And then begins this hideous cutting process.

The *Tennis* magazine cuts were particularly grievous, and at one point I remember getting into a bit of a tiff with the head editor, who's this, you know, Connecticut lady with a lot of yellow in her closet, I think. There was stuff about—you know, there was just certain ridiculous things the United States Tennis Association was doing. And I had had some stuff about that, and she wanted that cut, because it turns out the USTA is a big sponsor of the magazine, at which point I of course get to get on my little moral high horse and invoke the First Amendment and all that stuff.

It all got worked out. I remember the poor editor—what was this guy's name? Jennings, Jay Jennings—was just this poor—he was just right in the middle of this. And like me and the head editor just were like cats, fighting with each other. And he of course can't lose his job, but he also, you know, asked me to do this and feels obligated to me. But anyway, the whole thing ended up being, of course, fine.

Q: There are several places around the book where you have sort of a challenge to the editors. Where you're saying that they probably won't like this, or they'll cut this.

DFW: [Chuckles.] Yes.

Q: Were there some of those that didn't make it? That did get—

DFW: No, the deal with the book—the whole, really the reason for doing the book, other than the fact that Little, Brown said they'd publish it, and I of course am a whore, is that this was a chance to do kind of the long, original versions of these things that had just gone through meat grinders in various magazines. So the annoying-dash-amusing thing about the versions of the essays in the book is that they really do have 99 percent of the original stuff in them, including "I predict this will get cut by the editor." Because I knew this was an editor who had a big, blunt machete at the ready in his office and stuff. And I—

Q: Did any of those predictions make it into print in the *Harper's* version?

DFW: *Harper's*— Three of the things were done by *Harper's*, and *Harper's* does some cuts. But I think they cut better and they consult more with their writers. And I think they let a couple of those go in when they thought they were like amusing. But no, most of them, most of them, the editors would cut, with the very convincing rationale that, well, we have to cut 3,000 words, and is that particular footnote as important to you as something else? And I would say no. And that would be that.

Q: The thing about Andre Agassi looking like a Port Authority whore—

DFW: —I don't know—

Q: —didn't run in the original.

DFW: I think *Esquire*, *Esquire* did leave a couple of those in, and I remember my mom, you know, reading that and just, kind of, her eyes being very wide the next time she saw me. There was something about Brooke Shields looking like somebody you'd masturbate to a picture of but not have sex with, that was really one of those four-in-the-morning, 15-cup-of-coffee-really, if I'd been in my right mind, I wouldn't have put it in the final draft, but I did. And then *Esquire*, I remember, left it in. Being *Esquire*. You know, wanting to create as much unpleasantness as possible. So.

But anyway, I guess—I should go on the record as saying, there is really kind of a reason for the book, and the reason is probably somewhat juvenile, but it was that I'd worked really hard on these things and then magazines slice-and-diced 'em, and here was the chance to do kind of the director's cut.

You don't have to put in the thing about me being a whore. [Laughs.] By which I simply meant it's just a big thrill to have a publishing company be willing to publish one of your books. I'm getting in more trouble.

Q: How many words was the original version of the title

essay? And how many hours of work did that represent? Hours of writing time.

DFW: I don't know how many words. I mean, I remember, I always try to fool the magazine editors by sending stuff in with like single spaced and eight-point font.

Q: It's all counted on computers now, you know.

DFW: Which of course insults them, because they think, what, what, I think they're idiots? Like I think they don't recognize type? So then there's always this thing of like they call me up and get pissed, and I have to send it back in with 12-point font, double-spaced.

I think the cruise essay was about 110 pages, and I think it ended up getting cut just about in half. And every time I'd bitch and moan to *Harper's*, they would say, well, this is still, this is going to be the longest thing we've ever put in *Harper's*. At which point I would have to shut up or look like even a bigger prima donna than I am.

But no, that took—the cruise thing, let me see, I got done with that in March—ehhhh— The cruise thing took almost three months to do. And then it took another like two weeks of—I mean, I had to go to New York and sit in a room with the editor. We were cutting like widows and orphans off the ends of lines to get it to fit. It was very exciting. Rewrote the ending like an hour before they had to wrap the magazine. And so the typesetter's putting it in on their Quark system as the editor and I are rewriting it.

It was like that moment in *Broadcast News*—I don't know if you remember this—when Joan Cusack is having to run through the hallway to get the tape to Jack Nicholson in time to run it. Kind of my peak moment in the magazine industry. It was one I'll always remember.

Q: Was it like a totally different ending, or just a revision?

DFW: It was just, you know, as usual, *Harper's* editors, I like *Harper's* editors, I think they're real smart. And the editor said, "I don't think this ending works." And I of course fought with him and then finally knuckled under and did a new ending right there. And the ending, the end—he was right. The rewritten ending was a lot better.

And then the nice—the better ending ended up going in the book. Some of *Harper's* edits just made lines better and less clunky and less long, and so it's probably not quite honest to say this book is just exactly the way they were originally done. They were kind of the best blend of editors' cuts and the original thing.

I'm sorry, I feel like I'm not being particularly clear. I'm doing the best I can.

Q: That makes sense. Not to pry, but do they pay standard per-word scale for tens of thousands of words?

DFW: I don't think magazines—I think maybe the *New Yorker* pays by the word, but I've never done anything for the *New Yorker*. No, *Harper's* pays, *Harper's* pays I think like

2,500 or 3,000. See, *Harper's* pays less, but they fuck with your stuff less. That's the tradeoff with *Harper's*.

It's like in fiction, there's a trade-off between, you can publish stuff in literary journals, where they don't really pay you anything, but they also won't mess with the story. Whereas if you publish it in a glossy mag, you get more money, and it's I think a bigger ego thrill, but they also, then you're in for like four knock-down fights with fact-checkers and editors and all this stuff.

And *Harper's*, of the glossies, I think—I don't think they pay quite as much as the *Atlantic* and *New Yorker*, but they work with you rather than cram stuff down your throat. Which—eeugh, I don't mean to cast aspersions on the other magazines, it's just—I think *Harper's*, I don't think they're as rich, I don't think they have as much money as other magazines. They're kind of halfway between a glossy and kind of a literary magazine or something.

Other ones, no, you get like a couple thousand dollars for each one. There's not really very much money in it, I guess, unless you're one of these guys who's doing like one every two weeks, for *Sports Illustrated* or something.

Q: How do you handle being responsible for facts, writing nonfiction, after writing fiction? Coming to a genre where the things you say have to be on some level verifiably true?

DFW: That's a real good question. And the first one of these that I did, in order, the first one I did was the very first one, about playing tennis as a Midwesterner. Where I had some shit that I just, that was like impressionistic, and I didn't know, and I'd never dealt with a fact-checker before. And they're like, "We discovered there is no yacht and tennis club in Aurora, Illinois, what are we to do?" And I was like, oh, God.

So after that I just started to take better notes and be willing to back stuff up. The thing is, really—between you and me and the *Boston Phoenix*'s understanding readers— you hire a fiction writer to do nonfiction, there's going to be the occasional bit of embellishment.

Not to mention the fact that, like, when people tell you stuff, very often it comes out real stilted. If you just write down exactly what they said. And so you sort of have to rewrite it so it sounds more out-loud, which I think means putting in some "likes" or taking out some punctuation that the person might originally have said. And I don't really make any apologies for that.

Q: Also when you're writing about real events, there are other people who are at the same events. Have you heard back from the people that you're writing about? Trudy especially comes to mind—

DFW: [Groans]

Q: —who you described as looking like—

DFW: That, that was a very bad scene, because they were really nice to me on the cruise. And actually sent me a couple cards, and were looking forward to the thing coming out. And then it came out, and, you know, I never heard from them again. I feel—I'm worried that it hurt their feelings.

The. Thing. Is. Is, you know, saying that somebody looks like Jackie Gleason in drag, it might not be very nice, but if you just, if you could have seen her, it was true. It was just absolutely true. And so it's one reason why I don't do a lot of these, is there's a real delicate balance between fucking somebody over and telling the truth to the reader.

The Michael Joyce—what is that called? Oh, that's the one with the really long title in the book—was really, really upsetting. Can I tell you this? Yeah, I won't say the name of the magazine. That was originally commissioned by a different magazine. And I screwed up, because I really got to like this kid. There was some stuff about this kid that would have been very interesting in the article, that he, in kind of naked candor, told me, and then asked me not to print it. And, you know, and I didn't. And I wouldn't put it in.

But I, dickhead that I am, made the mistake of telling this magazine this. And they ended up killing the piece. So I never expected that piece even to see print, and then *Esquire*, I guess, an *Esquire* editor had a beer with the editor of this other magazine, and *Esquire* picked it up, even without, you know, the icky stuff about this guy.

Not icky like he did anything. There was just stuff that would have been embarrassing to him. The thing is, is I think if I was really a pro, I would have printed it. I mean, I'm not going to see the guy anymore. He's not—there wouldn't—I had it there in the notes, there wouldn't have been anything legal he could do. And then, I'm sure you've run into this, I sort of got, I got captured by this guy, and I really liked him.

One reason why I might have put in some not particularly kind stuff on the cruise is that I felt like I'd kind of learned my lesson. I wasn't going to hurt anybody or, you know, talk about anybody having sex with a White House intern or something. But I was going to tell the truth. And I couldn't just so worry about Trudy's feelings that I couldn't say the truth. Which is, you know, a terrific, really nice, and not unattractive lady who did happen to look just like Jackie Gleason in drag.

Q: Maybe if you'd emphasized that it was not in an unattractive way. Which is sort of a hard thing to picture.

DFW: Actually the first draft of that did have that, and the editor pointed out that not only did this waste words, but it looked like I was trying to have my cake and eat it too. That I was trying to tell an unkind truth but somehow give her a neck rub at the same time. So it got cut.

Q: But you actually did want to have your cake and eat it too. Not in a bad way.

DFW: I'm unabashed, I think, in wanting to have my cake and eat it too.

Q: The titles are different between the originals and the book.

DFW: God love magazines, but the editor picks the title, and they don't even really consult with you about it. And if you protest, they'll invoke house style, blah blah blah blah, a certain image for the magazine. There's just nothing you can do about it. But this was my revenge.

Q: Is there any chance of Celebrity Cruises picking some less negative passage out of the 'A Supposedly Fun Thing' essay and using the 'Shipping Out' title and reprinting it for promotion?

DFW: I believe A. I would have to give my consent, and I would not, because I think, there was a horrible sort of Frank Conroy thing—but B. they're not going to. They were not amused, and actually there was some litigatory saber-rattling with *Harper's*.

Which *Harper's*—these editors, you've really got to meet these guys—the editor of course, pointed out blandly out on the phone that 90 percent of this essay was going on and on about how almost insanity-producing luxurious and terrific Celebrity Cruises was. So they really kind of, they kind of had to stick their chest out but back down.

It wasn't like I was saying, you know, that they were dumping toxic waste over the side or anything. I just said that I was worried they were going to try to assassinate me with a toilet. I came off, I think, far sort of more pathetic in that thing than Celebrity Cruises did. But anyway, the chances, I think, of them—I don't know.

I don't know whether you're interested. This is kind of

funny. At the beginning, I was talking to, Celebrity Cruises has the services of some kind of PR company or somebody, somebody who does their press releases and stuff. And *Harper's* got me the number of this lady. Who I think is quoted in the piece.

Q: Yeah.

DFW: And it started out real good. You know, it started out like real, she's very helpful and all this stuff. And then, as it got on, and she started to bristle at some of the questions—and then toward the end, she started shunting me over to this vice president of this PR who was this lady who, like, you could just tell ate Rocky Mountain oysters for breakfast, it was just like.

And she began, you know, sort of like, "We want to see a copy of this," "We want to make sure you're not going to libel us," or whatever. It just got really, really amusing. And it was tempting to put some of that stuff in, but it was too, it was just unrelated to the cruise itself. But they were not pleased.

Q: Have you heard from Frank Conroy since you wrote that?

DFW: I'm trying to remember what happened. The sad thing about the Conroy thing is, Conroy was real decent to me on the phone. I basically said to him, "I've got some problems with this, I want to hear your justification." And then he said, you know, he said what he said, and I printed what he said.

And I seem to remember—I don't think I talked to him or he sent me a note, but he and I know some people in common, and I think I had through them conveyed not really an apology, but just regrets, and hope that this thing didn't cause him too much pain. And that he conveyed back, no problem, or something like that.

That was a tough one, because I've got no, you know, this guy's kind of a hero of mine 'cause of *Stop Time*. I got no interest in doing him any harm. And yet I think what he did was wrong.

Q: Besides Conroy, are there any nonfiction writers who inspired your work, or—?

DFW: Oh, golly. Ever since I was in college, I've been an enormous fan of both Joan Didion and Pauline Kael. And I don't know—I think prosewise, Pauline Kael is unequaled. I mean, maybe McPhee, at his very best, is as good.

And so I don't know what influence they have, but in terms of just being slobbering fans of? Conroy's first book, Tobias Wolff, Tobias Wolff, *This Boy's Life*. Oh, God. There's a book by a mathematician named Hardy at Oxford called *A Mathematician's Apology*.

Hardy gets mentioned in *Good Will Hunting*, by the way. Have you seen that movie?

Q: No.

DFW: Oh. Well, there's a brief mention of Hardy. Anyway. There are quite a few that are just really really really really good. But I'd say Pauline Kael above all of them is sort of, I think, the best. Annie Dillard's really good, but she's much more sort of restrained.

Q: Did you see her essay in the *Harper's* where 'The Depressed Person' ran?

DFW: Yeah. I thought it was a real sort of one-two punch of holiday cheer. The bizarre thing about that, man, is that they were going to run it a month earlier, and they said, oh, no, we don't want to run it in our Christmas issue, it's too depressing. So they wait and run it in the January issue, which happens to come to everybody's house like 10 days before Christmas.

So it's like, I don't know. I don't know what they were thinking.

That was a kind of a weird Dillard essay, but it's certainly Dillard. She's got that one about them watching the deer tied to the tree dying in South America. You know the one I'm talking about?

Q: Yeah.

DFW: That's just—it raises hair on your body. In places you don't even have hair.

How many words you got on this thing, by the way?

Q: For this piece? I don't know. We're just going to transcribe it and see what happens.

DFW: Have you ever—I mean, you go through the cuts process, right?

Q: Oh, yeah.

DFW: You chew your knuckle.

Q: Yes.

DFW: Yes. So you know what I'm talking about.

Q: Absolutely.

DFW: Yeah.

Q: Yeah, early on, I had a piece reduced by about 70 percent.

DFW: So you know what I mean, then, about like *Harper's*, you know, the editors, actually, some of the time, make your stuff better in the cuts. You just, you get real attached to 'em. 'Cause it's so easy to mangle. Or like, oh, we want to put in another Gap ad, let's cut four paragraphs. That stuff just makes you upset.

Q: Yeah. Absolutely.

DFW: I used to read the *Phoenix*, by the way. Religiously. When I was there.

Q: Oh, really? That's good to know.

DFW: This is a bit of a tickle for me.

Q: So what did you think of *Good Will Hunting*?

DFW: Aaah. I think it's the ultimate nerd fantasy movie. I think it's a bit of a fairy tale, but I enjoyed it a lot, and Minnie Driver is really to fall sideways for.

And there's all kinds of cool stuff. It's actually a movie that's got calculus in it, you know. Takes place in Boston. There's all kinds of—one guy I talked to who saw it described it as a cross between *Ordinary People* and *The Computer Wore Tennis Shoes*, which I thought was kind of funny. And if you see it, you'll see, that's not un-germane. [Chuckles.]

Do you remember that movie? Are you old enough to remember *The Computer Wore Tennis Shoes*?

Q: *The Computer Wore Tennis Shoes*? No.

DFW: It's got Kurt Russell. There's an electrical accident. In the computer room, when he's this student in some college. It's like, you know, the old sci-fi, you know, toxic-accident-turns-him-into-Spider-Man thing. So he gets shocked, and these are great old computers with like reel-to-reel tapes running back and forth. And it apparently injects him with every bit of data known to man. And he goes on *College Bowl*. It's got Joe Flynn. It's got a lot of people. You should check it out. Disney. I think um '69, '70.

Q: Yep, that was before my time.

DFW: Yeah, well, the miracle of videotape.

Q: Yes. The *Phoenix* reviewer who handled *A Supposedly Fun Thing* wrote that your style "distills the contemporary speech of under-40, middle-class Americans. The way Wallace writes is the way I'll remember having spoken." And you've been hailed in a lot of places in a generational spokesman.

DFW: Hailed?

Q: Hailed? Sure. Or "described." How do you feel about that role?

DFW: I, eh, I don't know. I can remember being on some, doing some radio thing in Boston a couple years ago, and somebody calling in and asking me about being the spokesman for, like, Generation X. Which I think I'm a little too old to be, anyway. But the whole thing just seems absurd, because sort of the—How old are you?

Q: Uh, 26.

DFW: Oh, OK, so much more for you. I mean, I'm 35, and I think for the generation that starts with me or a couple years younger, the whole defining thing is that there can be no spokesman. It's completely atomized, and there's nothing like a kind of unified consciousness the way there was, I don't know, in the '60s, or even during that kind of conservative spasm in the '80s.

And so the whole idea of a spokesman for a generation distinguished for the fact that it's anomic and atomized and alienated is just, is silly. I like stuff that sounds intimate to me, and that sounds like almost there's somebody talkin' in my ear. And I think at least some of the stuff that I do tries to sound out-loud, aural, you know, with an A-U. R-A-L. I mean, Jesus, you know, people were doing that and trying to do that 200 years ago. Like it's anything very new.

Q: How much art goes into creating the artless effect?

DFW: I don't understand what you mean by that?

Q: Trying to make it sound natural and to achieve the effect of—

DFW: I don't know. I think it's—the accurate answer is the vague one. Sometimes it's fairly easy. And other times it isn't. I think a very interesting case of this is Don DeLillo, who I think does the best dialogue like of anybody alive.

And if you read DeLillo dialogue, it's funny, because it sounds very real and very natural, but if you go back and look at it, it's really not. You know, it's kind of like, um, there will be a line where somebody says, "I'm only saying." And then there's the next line, so your eye's got to track over the right space and then go down to the next line, and there's a much longer pause than in a real conversation, when, if you and I are having an argument, and I'd say, "I'm only sayin'—" and then you cut me off?

Q: Mm-hm.

DFW: I don't know if I'm making any sense. So in a way, it really isn't, it isn't natural at all. And I think it's a very kind of affected, arty thing to do. The trick, though, is when the reader gets reading quickly, and there's kind of that brain voice starts? Like somebody talking to you? It ends up sounding very natural. And that's something that seems to me to be very interesting.

Q: In your own stuff, the footnotes have a way of making the reader kind of break stride, or have to leap around and backtrack, instead of just proceeding on through the works linearly. One thing about reading the footnote-intensive stuff of yours is that usually, I'm pretty good at, when I go back to a piece, finding something spatially on the page.

DFW: Uh-huh?

Q: Like I know it's on a left-hand page toward the bottom. But that doesn't happen. Like I get lost in your stuff. How hard do you want the reader to have to work?

DFW: You know what? To be honest with you, it's not some-thing that I—I don't really think that way, and I don't think that way because I just don't, I don't want to go down that path of trying to anticipate, like a chess player, every read-er's reaction.

The footnotes, the honest thing is, is the footnotes were an intentional, programmatic part of *Infinite Jest*, and they get to be kind of—you get sort of addicted to 'em. And for me, a lot of those pieces were written around the time that I was typing and working on *Infinite Jest*, and so it's just, it's a kind of loopy way of thinking, that it seems to me is in some ways mimetic.

I don't know you, but certainly the way I think about things and experience things is not particularly linear, and it's not orderly, and it's not pyramidical, and there are a lot of loops. Most of the nonfiction pieces are basically, just, look, I'm not a great journalist, and I can't interview any-body, but what I can do is kind of, I will slice open my head for you. And let you see a cross-section of just a kind of average, averagely bright person's head at this thing.

And in a way, the footnotes, I think, are better rep-resentations of, not really stream-of-consciousness, but thought patterns and fact patterns. How exactly different readers read them—I mean, I've talked to people who wait and read the footnotes at the end, or who do them abso-lutely the way they're numbered.

I think the only thing for me, the tricky thing with the footnotes, is that they are an irritant, and they require a little extra work, and so they either have to be really ger-mane or they have to be kind of fun to read.

It does get to be a problem, though, when I'm like, every single gag that occurs to me I think I can toss into the thing, and toss it in as a footnote. And the most heavily cut thing in the book was the David Lynch essay. I mean, the book editor had me cut like a third of it, and a lot of it was just footnotes that are just gags. And I think he has a good point.

Q: How much gag writing do you do? To what extent when you're doing these things do you try to be deliberately humorous, and how much do comic effects just sort of arise from the thought processes?

DFW: I'll tell you. I think another reason why I'm not doing any more of these for a while is, by the end, I think the last one I did was the Lynch thing, there really was kind of a shtick emerging. And the shtick was somewhat neurotic, hyper-conscious guy, like, showing you how weird this thing is that not everybody thinks is weird.

I think it's more that kind of trying to—trying to notice stuff that everybody else notices but they don't really notice that they notice? Which I think a fair amount of good comedians do that, too. I don't think, I would never go, oh, it's time for a gag, and just stick in a gag or something.

Or if I did, it would end up getting cut. Because, you know, if it's just gratuitous, then the reader's going to throw the book at the wall.

I'm not giving that a very clear answer. That's as close to the truth as I can come.

Q: I mean, when you have something like the oil rigs "bobbing fellatially"—

DFW: Yeah, except that's exactly how they look. [Laughs]

Q: It is exactly how they look, but it also—that's funny enough to—

DFW: But that was another, that was a big fight, 'cause I originally had "fellatically," which I thought sounded better, it had more of a harsh, glottal, fellatiatory sound, and then the copy editor goes, there's no such word, we've got to say "fellatially," and I think that sounds like "palatially," and I don't like it. I mean, 48 hours are spent thumb-wrestling over this bullshit.

Q: Yeah, no, that happens. You think that you've just sort of Shakespearianally come up with a different word form—

DFW: Yes.

Q: —and then somewhere there's a copy editor who—

DFW: Yes.

Q: —informs you that you've got it wrong.

DFW: Yes. I don't know where they—well, some of them are really good. But some of them are just anal. To the max.

Now I'm trying to figure out whether any of them are going to read this.

Q: How much distance is there between David Foster Wallace—the narrator—and yourself?

DFW: I don't understand the question?

Q: How crafted is that persona? Because it has the appearance of course of, like, nakedness, and an actual opening up of the thought process. But at the same time, you said, like with the David Lynch thing, you felt it sort of turning into shtick.

DFW: Yeeeah. Well. Huh. You know, I think sincerity can be a shtick. I know people, just in private life—you know the kind of person who takes great pride that they will never have an unuttered thought, and there will never be a truth, you know, they're like, "So how do I look in this?" "Wellll, I'd love to tell you you look good, but I've just gotta tell the truth, you look awful"—you know what I mean, those people?

Q: Mm-hmm.

DFW: And uh—[sighs]. The hard thing about any of this stuff is, after a while, almost anything becomes this kind of postmodern pose. And I think really the first four or five of those, particularly like through the cruise, I don't think there was really any persona there at all, except what emerged through the fact the thing was getting cut over and over again, and I'd cut out the lines that were clunky or whatever. I don't think anybody thinks entertainingly at all times.

By the end, like by the Lynch thing, I began to kind of hear that voice in my head that I thought of as the nonfiction shtick voice. I don't think I particularly like the idea of having a persona in nonfiction. I think it's basically the heart of fiction, but I don't really like that idea in nonfiction, particularly nonfiction that's trying to slice open its brain for you.

And that might be another reason to cut it out for a while.

The natural hope is that if you don't write any more nonfiction for four or five years, you'll sort of be a different person, and that voice and sensibility will be different by the time you go back to it. With any luck.

Q: So what are you working on now?

DFW: When you were in college, did you read much Parmenides? The pre-Socratic?

Q: No.

DFW: Parmenides has this very interesting thing about, what does not exist yet cannot coherently be spoken of? It's like contradictory?

Q: OK.

DFW: I invoke Parmenides.

Q: OK. Did you read much Parmenides when you were in college?

DFW: We had to—I remember spending months and months on the pre-Socratics. We had a prof who was really big on the pre-Socratics.

Q: What was your major?

DFW: I was a—well, actually, I'm not sure if I had enough math to be a math major. I think my book majors were philosophy and English.

Q: OK.

DFW: I might have been a triple—I don't think I ever declared math. A lot of philosophy classes, like logic and semantics and number theory and stuff are kind of both philosophy and math.

Q: So you said there was a period of time, like six days, when you were really hot with magazine editors. How's the whole pendulum of fame swinging?

DFW: The degree of fame we're talking about here—getting hot as a writer for six days is equivalent to a fan base of like a local TV weatherman, right? Magazines are certainly not calling every day to ask me to do stuff anymore, which to be honest is something of a relief, 'cause there's other stuff I'm working on.

I don't—see, the thing about it, I've been doing this since the mid-'80s. Since the mid-'80s, I've watched, you know, I don't know how many writers get hot, and then not get hot, and then get hot again, and then not get hot, and you just—after a while, you just kind of don't really take it seriously? A lot of it is just kind of the peristalsis of the industry.

The industry I think it's so pressed, and so anxious to create kind of heat and buzz around specific people, you know? It's the same way movies are, the same way music is. Although the amounts of money at stake in books are vanishingly small.

It's nice when the phone doesn't ring as much, and it's not very good for me when people treat me like a big shot. Because then I get puffed up inside. But other than that, it doesn't really make much difference?

Q: How big does the big-shot treatment get?

DFW: Oh, I just mean—giving a reading, I remember giving a reading in the late '80s, and like nobody came. I remember giving a reading at, it wasn't the Harvard Bookstore, but it was a bookstore in Harvard, and it was December of '91, and *Harper's* had this whole idea that they were going to put on these readings of people reading their stuff from the magazine. And this was when that one about playing tennis as a kid came out.

And the *Harper's* PR person came to Boston and I came and I gave that reading, and it was, I mean, nobody showed up. There was like a snowstorm, but. The basic point is nobody showed up. And so me and the PR guy went out and ate like three pieces of cake each and apologized to each other for three hours.

So, being used to that kind of stuff, you know, giving a reading in New York and having some people not be able to get in is just, is weird, and I think it makes you feel like you're a big shot. Temporarily. The Sauron-like eye of the culture passes over you, like in *Lord of the Rings*. You're old enough to know *Lord of the Rings*. A bitchingly good read, I think.

Q: There's one other thing that I wanted to ask you about, which was the relationship between footnotes and hypertext.

DFW: I've had people say that, and I would love them to think that there's some grand theory. I sometimes use a computer to type when I've got a lot of corrections to do, but I don't have a modem, I've never been on the Internet. There's a guy in my department who teaches hypertext, but I don't really know anything about it.

Q: You do your stuff by typewriter?

DFW: I mostly typewrite. Some of the magazine stuff I did on disk, because you learn that the magazines very often will ask for a disk. And there's this great term they use: they say, Well, we'll just take the disk and massage it. I still can't get them to be entirely clear what "massage" means. I guess it means, like, changing the formats or something. I think it's a terrific term to use for a disk.

But basically, I can type and I can save stuff onto disk, and that's just about it, in terms of computers. I feel like an old fogy.

Good luck on this. You're going to exceed whatever word limit, I'll bet.

Q: Yeah. Well, we're just going to take the whole tape and, you know, cut it down into something that—

DFW: Just massage the tape.

Q: We're going to massage the tape.

DFW: Cool.

A BRIEF INTERVIEW WITH A FIVE-DRAFT MAN

INTERVIEW BY STACEY SCHMEIDEL

FIRST PUBLISHED IN *AMHERST MAGAZINE*

SPRING 1999

1) This interview-by-mail is an unusual medium for an *Amherst* magazine interview. From your perspective, what are the benefits of presenting you and your work to readers this way?

I am a Five Draft man. I actually learned this at Amherst, in William Kennick's Philosophy 17 and 18, with their brutal paper-every-two-weeks schedules. I got down a little system of writing and two rewrites and two typed drafts. I've used it ever since. I like it. My problem with most interviews is that they're terribly first-draftish. If an interview question is even remotely interesting, it's going to be hard to answer it briefly. I always wish they'd let me scuttle into the next room and do five drafts and come back out. This way, unless it turns out your deadline's real short, I can do five drafts. Actually this is better for everybody, because the more drafts I have the more succinct I can be (usually).

2) You were a talented tennis player and an outstanding student at Urbana High School in Illinois. What brought you to Amherst?

I was a marginally talented tennis player as a teenager. I got hurt freshman year (Sp. '81), but I probably wouldn't have made the Amherst varsity anyway; there were at least two other freshmen who were clearly better than I. People tend to think I'm a better player than I really am.

Nor was I an outstanding student in high school. I wasn't anywhere near the top of my class, anyway. I was sort of too much a jock to be a really first-rate student and a little too nerdy to make a good jock.

My father is an Amherst alumnus, and he also teaches at a big public university. The sum total of his college-application advice was that small liberal arts schools tended to be better for undergrads. So I visited several small LAS schools, of which Amherst was one. What I hadn't known was that if you were the child of an alumnus, the Admissions guy would tell you right in the interview whether they'd take you or not. *[Editor's note: This no longer is true.]* This is a huge perk, it seems to me, given the amount of hand-wringing and knuckle-biting my high-school classmates had to go through. Anyway, this perk, plus a laziness that made me not even bother applying anyplace else, is what brought me to Amherst.

3) How will people who knew you at Amherst remember you?

4) How do you remember Amherst? What are the experiences—in and out of the classroom—that shape those memories?

5) Similarly, what aspects of your Amherst education served you best? And what are the things about Amherst that, in hindsight, disappoint you?

I don't know that many would remember me at all. For one thing, I had a tendency to take semesters off and stay home, so I started out as '84 and ended as '85. For another thing, I was cripplingly shy at Amherst. I wasn't in a fraternity and didn't go to parties and didn't have much to do with the life of the College. I had a few very close friends and that was it. I studied all the time. I mean literally all the time. I was one of those people they had to flicker the lights of Frost Library to get out of there on Friday nights who'd be out there right after brunch on Sunday waiting on the steps for them to open the doors.

There were happy reasons for all this studying, and sad reasons. It was at Amherst, with its high expectations and brilliant profs and banzai workload, that I loved to read and write and think. In many ways I came alive there. But I was always terrified. Amherst terrified me—the beauty of it, the tradition, the elitism, the expense. But it was less Amherst than me: I was a late bloomer and still deeply in adolescence when I entered college. I had an adolescent's radical self-absorption, and my particular self-absorption manifested as terror and inadequacy. This is the sad part. The same obsessive studying that helped me come alive also kept me dead: it was a way to hide from people, to try to earn—through 'achievement' or whatever—permission to

be at Amherst that I was too self-centered to realize I'd already received when they accepted me.

So 'the things about Amherst that, in hindsight, disappoint [me]' are things not about Amherst but about who I
was when I was there. I let almost no one know me, and I
lost the chance to know and learn from most of my peers. It
took years after I'd graduated from Amherst to realize that
people were actually far more complicated and interesting
than books, that almost everyone else suffered the same se-
cret fears and inadequacies as I, and that feeling alone and
inferior was actually the great valent bond between us all. I
wish I'd been smart enough to understand that when I was
an adolescent.

6) You did two honor theses at Amherst. What on earth
were you thinking?

My very best friend at Amherst, Mark Costello '84, had
done two the year before, one a piece of fiction. So there
was precedent. Plus I was having a hard time deciding
whether to go to grad school in philosophy or writing, and
it seemed like a good idea to try doing sustained work in
both and seeing which I liked better. (The option of not going to grad school *at all* didn't occur to me; that's how much
an academic brat I was at the time.) Plus I didn't exactly
have huge demands on my time during senior year, since
most of my closest friends had graduated the spring before.
Anyway, it turns out that a thesis isn't any more work than
two hard classes—and we got one class per semester off

for thesis work. The trick was starting early, in September instead of February. I'd watched several friends put themselves through hell the year before by futzing around the first semester, so I started early, and it wasn't that hard.

7) Amherst is an institution that places a high value on the written word. Your writing is consistently singled out for its distinctive voice. To what extent was your writing style influenced by the courses you took and by the professors and students you met at Amherst? (Also, what influences outside of Amherst do you credit with shaping your style?)

Praise is always nice, but I don't really feel like there's anything terribly distinctive or original about the 'voice' of my stuff. Most of the modern writing I like the best is both sophisticated and colloquial—that is, high-level and complicated but at the same time intimate, sort of like a smart person is sitting right there talking to you—and I think I do little more than try to achieve this same high-low blend. Just having to write paper after paper—more writing my freshman year at Amherst than I'd done in three years of high school—and having first-rate adult minds respond to my stuff (I can still remember the wonderfully dry acerbic little comments that profs like [William] Kennick and [John] Cameron and [Alan] Parker and [Dale] Peterson would put in the margins when I tried to BS or be too cute)...all this helps.

8) Can you talk about your writing process? When/where/ how do you write? Do you rewrite?

Well, like I said, I am a Five Draft man...the first two of these drafts are pen-and-paper, which is a bit old-fashioned, but other than that I don't think there's anything very distinctive about my work habits. I fluctuate between periods of terrible sloth and paralysis and periods of high energy and production, but from what I know about other writers this isn't unusual. Work-wise, my only real distinction is that I am an incredibly fast and accurate two-finger typist, the best I've ever heard of (another skill honed at A.C.).

9) Amherst magazine likes to profile alumni whose work has had an impact on the world outside of Amherst. How would you describe the impact of your work? (That may be a two-part question: What kind of impact do you hope your work will have as you're creating it? And what do you think the actual impact has been?) And how do you measure the success of your work?

Sneaky, Ms. S.: this question actually comprises more than two subquestions. And unfortunately this is all stuff that I've discovered it's in my own best interests not to think much about. 'Impact' is tricky because it has so much to do with interpretation and fashion (which phenomena are far from independent of each other). Plus plain luck: the fact that you've got to find first an agent and then an editor and then an editor's publishing co. who not only like your stuff but believe it to be 'viable'—which in 1999 America means salable in sufficient numbers to permit an approximate 7-percent net profit—before you even get to consider something like 'impact' the way Q9's using it. And I know way too many fine and serious writers who haven't been able to get anything published to be able to regard the whole process as anything much more than a lottery. Then, if your thing does get published, and if some combination of cultural kismet and corporate hype garners it an audience, you get to discover how extremely remote people's takes on your work are from anything you had in mind when you were working on it, plus how little whatever they feel and think about the work's author has to do with you as you know and experience yourself. . .

I've hit on an effective way to handle all this schizogenic stuff, which is to keep the whole thing at a very simple level, roughly a level/vocabulary that an average US fifth-grader can understand. I want my work to be good. I want to like it. This is the only part that has anything to do with me. I can't make it have an 'impact' on anybody else. This doesn't mean I can't hope it has one, but I can't do anything to guarantee it, or even to cause it. All I can do is make something as good as I can make it (this is the sort of fact that's both banal and profound), and promise myself that I'll never try to publish anything I myself don't think is good or finished. I used to have far more complex and sophisticated ways of thinking about 'impact,' but they always left me with my forehead against the wall.

10) You've received attention for both fiction and non-fiction work. What do you see as the merits and drawbacks of each genre?

I think of myself as a fiction writer. The nonfiction thing is a result of a patronage of a *Harper's* editor named Colin Harrison who in the early '90s started dreaming up marvelous little experiential assignments for me, mostly I think to keep me alive (I was really, really poor in the early '90s, though this was mostly my own fault), and then also helped shape them, etc., and they got a good response, etc. etc. And the interesting thing about the US magazine industry is that it runs almost entirely on Herd Instinct, so that if one or two things in *Harper's* turn out well, editors at all sorts of other magazines start calling and pitching prose-intensive experiential non-fiction assignments, and even if you take only one in a hundred of these offers (offers that flood in during the interval in which you are considered 'hot' by a couple dozen editors who must surely go through one another's mail), there are still enough for a book pretty quickly... especially considering that magazines will always (a) lavishly overpay you and then (b) feel free to chop and mangle the hell out of your piece before it runs, ignoring your squeaks of protest because it turns out the lavish payment in (a) bought them the right to chop and mangle, which everyone in the Industry appears to understand but you.

11) Much of your work has to do with our seemingly

insatiable need for instant gratification through passive en-
joyment of entertainment. Can you talk about the chal-
lenges of looking critically at entertainment media while
also trying to provide an experience that is—at base level,
anyway—entertaining? Why do you choose this medium
to deliver this message?

Unanswerable within the constraints of a condensed back-
and-forth like this (see Q14).

12) Do you read reviews of your work?

It's tempting to. It's also tempting to try and eavesdrop on
people who are talking about you and don't think you can
hear them. But you almost always get your feelings hurt if
you eavesdrop like this. It's the same way with reviews. It
took me a while to figure out that reviews of my work are
not *for* me. They're for potential book-buyers. I have a nice
tight established circle of friends and associates I can send
stuff to and get honest critical response that helps me make
the stuff better. By the time the stuff is published, though,
anything I hear about it amounts to me eavesdropping.

13) What writers move you?

The question's verb is tricky. I regard Cynthia Ozick, Cormac McCarthy, and Don DeLillo as pretty much the
country's best living fiction writers (with Joanna Scott and
Richard Powers and Denis Johnson and Steve Erickson

being the cream of the country's Younger crop). But that's not quite what you're asking. I'm not sure I want to respond to what you're asking. 'Move' is tricky. I heard all kinds of sneery stuff about the book *Bridges of Madison Country* when it came out, and joined in the sneering, and then saw the movie version on an airplane and bawled my head off at the end, which was mortifying. I find the part of *It's a Wonderful Life* when Jimmy Stewart is yelling at Donna Reed that he doesn't want to get married and stuck in dreary airless little Beford Falls and at the same time hugging her and kissing on her and crying and saying '*Mara, Mara!*' tremendously moving. I find the end of *Lord of the Rings* when Frodo says 'I have been too badly wounded, Sam' moving. Etc. There's some top-shelf literary fiction I find moving—David Markson's *Wittgenstein's Mistress* is one, and Power's *Operation Wandering Soul*—but it's more a more complicated kind of 'moving' because this stuff involves cerebration and aesthetic apprehension and so on. Cerebration may produce a richer and more sophisticated kind of 'moving' but it's not the kind of stomach-punching emotion I guess I associate with 'move.' The truth is I don't think I've ever found anything as purely 'moving' as the end of *The Velveteen Rabbit* when I first read it.

14) What's the one question you always wish interviews would ask?

There really aren't any. The problem with interviews (including even very considerate ones where you let me write

answers out instead of just saying them) is that no truly interesting question can be satisfactorily answered within the
formal constraints (*viz.* magazine-space, radio-time, public decorum) of an interview. At least that's what I end up
feeling. It kind of puzzles me that people seem so keen on
asking fiction writers straightforward interview-type questions, since if the fiction writers really thought interesting
stuff could be talked about straightforwardly they probably
wouldn't have become fiction writers.

15) What were your aspirations when you left Amherst?
And what are they today?

This is a good example of the Q14 phenomenon. Questions
like this almost *demand* a quick pithy burst of pious meth-
ane. The fact that we'd need four pages of back-and-forth
to nail down exactly what you mean by 'aspirations' before
I could even start trying to answer you... and this would
not be pithy or brief or probably even very interesting to
anybody else. I'm 99+ percent sure you'd have the same
problem if somebody asked you, Ms. S., the question in
any kind of compressed public forum. Why do we do these
sorts of things to one another?

"TO TRY EXTRA HARD TO EXERCISE PATIENCE, POLITENESS, AND IMAGINATION"

INTERVIEW BY DAVE EGGERS

FIRST PUBLISHED IN *THE BELIEVER*

NOVEMBER 2003

David Foster Wallace is from east-central Illinois, and this is a large part of his appeal. In addition, he has written a number of books. Among them are the story collections *Girl with Curious Hair* and *Brief Interviews with Hideous Men*, and the novels *The Broom of the System* and *Infinite Jest*. There is also *A Supposedly Fun Thing I'll Never Do Again*, a collection of journalism and essays. It's fair to say that Wallace has shown himself to be capable of tackling any subject or genre he chooses; his versatility and his attention to detail—of the physical world and also the nuances of feeling and consciousness—have made him one of the most influential writers the United States has produced in the last twenty years. After spending many years living in Bloomington, Illinois, and teaching at Illinois State University—the sometime rival of but not the same as the University of Illinois—Wallace accepted in 2001 a position as Roy E. Disney Professor of English at Pomona College, in southern California. October marks the release of *Everything and More: A Compact History of* ∞. Below is an email exchange with Wallace, though it wasn't quite that. Questions were emailed to Wallace, who then took them home, answered them on his home computer—which is not connected to the Internet—printed those answers, and put them in the mail. As you can see, the interview could have and maybe should have gone on much longer. Wallace and his interviewer were traveling a lot in the weeks before this issue went to press, so we did our best. I guess it is six thousand words or so. That's a good length.

—*Dave Eggers*

THE BELIEVER: I guess it would be fitting enough to start by asking what prompted you to write this book, *Everything and More*. Was it your idea, or were you asked by the [W. W. Norton] Great Discoveries series to address the subject? And if you can answer this, you'd mentioned on the phone that you wrote *Everything and More* "two books ago," implying that there are two more finished Dave Wallace books in your desk drawer. Can you talk about those?

DAVID FOSTER WALLACE: I'll give you the short version. This is basically the same publishing outfit that had done Penguin Lives, and they were doing a new series where non-tech people wrote about seminal stuff in math and science, and they tracked me down in Texas (long story) and pitched me in I think the summer of 2000. I'd had a certain amount of philosophy of math in school, and had kept reading (unsystematically) in the field as a sort of half-assed hobby, so the idea of doing some nonfiction about math was not unappealing. (There's some grim and incidental data about how poorly other work was going in the summer of 2000, and how welcome was the idea of doing something else for a while, that for the most part I'll skip.)

I'd also had an office at Illinois State just down the hall from a guy who taught technical writing, and from reading some of his classes' materials and eavesdropping on his student conferences I'd gotten interested in tech writing and the rhetoric of technical info. At first I think the Series people's idea was that I was going to do Gödel and the Incompleteness Theorems, but then it switched to Cantorian set theory because I'd actually had a set theory class in school once, and to be honest I thought I could pretty much knock the thing off in four or five months. Except—for a variety of reasons that won't fit in this short version—it turned out that the only way to present the whole thing interestingly or in a way that hadn't been done before was to try to explain not just what Cantorian set theory was and how it worked but exactly where it came from, which given the essential transitivity of where things come from eventually meant going all the way back to Zeno and Aristotle et al. and tracing out the ways Western math had tried and failed to deal with ∞ from ancient Greece up through nineteenth-century analysis. All of which ended up taking a lot longer than five months, let me tell you.

BLVR: Before we go deeper into infinity, let's back up a second and talk about where this book fits into your other stuff. Your books so far are all recognizable as yours, unmistakably so, but on the other hand you haven't revisited the same structural territory more than once. You've written two novels, but they're not similar in too many ways, at least in terms of their overall architecture. Similarly, *Girl* *with Curious Hair* and *Brief Interviews* are both collections of stories, but are wildly different, sharing arguably little structural DNA. You've written journalism, and essays, and now this new book about infinity. But rarely have you seemed to go back into forms you've already explored. I haven't, for example, seen any journalism from you since the John McCain piece [in *Rolling Stone*]. Maybe the question I have is this: Once you've explored a form, like the short story for example, do you reach a point where you think you've exhausted its possibilities, and thus have to move on? Or are you sampling many different forms before inevitably revisiting all of them?

DFW: Here's an example of a question that's deeper and more interesting than my response can be. I know that the reason has nothing to do with feeling that a form's been exhausted. Actually, I don't understand the whole concept of form and forms very well, nor the various ways different forms and genres get distinguished and classified. Nor do I much care, really. My basic MO is that I tend to start and/or work on a whole lot of different things at the same time, and at a certain point they either come alive (to me) or they don't. Well over half of them do not, and I lack the discipline/fortitude to work for very long on something that feels dead, so they get abandoned, or put in a trunk, or stripped for parts for other things. It's all rather chaotic, or feels that way to me. What anybody else ever gets to see of mine, writing-wise, is the product of a kind of Darwinian struggle in which only things that are emphatically alive to me are worth finishing, fixing, editing, copyediting, page-proof-tinkering, etc. (I know you know this drill, and know the soul-fatigue of having to go over your own shit time after time for publication.) And it may be that in order to be really alive for me, a book-length thing has got to be different, feel different, than other stuff I've done... Or, on the other hand, my whole answer here might be hooey: The new book of stories is not all that different, structurally, from *GWCH,* or from most other story collections.

BLVR: You mention this book of stories again, but we haven't discussed it. Did you want to talk about it? I don't know anything about it. Up to you.

DFW: By all means let's discuss it. It's a book of stories. The shortest is 1.5 pages and the longest about 100. It was due last January 1 and I was six months late with it. Barring some sort of editorial disaster, it ought to come out next spring.

BLVR: You covered John McCain for the 2000 election, and that piece, which was so fresh and honest and unvarnished, was made into a kind of book-on-demand. Do you keep up with politics, and if so, are there plans to do any more political writing? And do you have any comment on why, it seems, there are fewer young novelists around who also comment directly on the political world? Should novelists be offering their opinions on national affairs, politics, our current and future wars?

DFW: The reason why doing political writing is so hard right now is probably also the reason why more young (am I included in the range of this predicate anymore?) fiction writers ought to be doing it. As of 2003, the rhetoric of the enterprise is fucked. 95 percent of political commentary, whether spoken or written, is now polluted by the very politics it's supposed to be about. Meaning it's become totally ideological and reductive: The writer/speaker has certain political convictions or affiliations, and proceeds to filter all reality and spin all assertion according to those convictions and loyalties. Everybody's pissed off and exasperated and impervious to argument from any other side. Opposing viewpoints are not just incorrect but contemptible, corrupt, evil. Conservative thinkers are balder about this kind of attitude: Limbaugh, Hannity, that horrific O'Reilly person. Coulter, Kristol, etc. But the Left's been infected, too. Have you read this new Al Franken book? Parts of it are funny, but it's totally venomous (like, what possible response can rightist pundits have to Franken's broadsides but further rage and return-venom?). Or see also e.g. Lapham's latest *Harper's* columns, or most of the stuff in the *Nation,* or even *Rolling Stone.* It's all become like Zinn and Chomsky but without the immense bodies of hard data these older guys use to back up their screeds. There's no more complex, messy, community-wide argument (or "dialogue"); political discourse is now a formulaic matter of preaching to one's own choir and demonizing the opposition. Everything's relentlessly black-and-whitened. Since the truth is way, way more gray and complicated than any one ideology can capture, the whole thing seems to me not just stupid but stupefying. Watching O'Reilly v. Franken is watching bloodsport. How can any of this possibly help me, the average citizen, deliberate about whom to choose to decide my country's macroeconomic policy, or how even to conceive for myself what that policy's outlines should be, or how to minimize the chances of North Korea nuking the DMZ and pulling us into a ghastly foreign war, or how to balance domestic security concerns with civil liberties? Questions like these are all massively complicated, and much of the complication is not sexy, and well over 90 percent of political commentary now simply abets the uncomplicatedly sexy delusion that one side is Right and Just and the other Wrong and Dangerous. Which is of course is a pleasant delusion, in a way—as is the belief that every last person you're in conflict with is an asshole—but it's childish, and totally unconducive to hard thought, give and take, compromise, or the ability of grown-ups to function as any kind of community.

My own belief, perhaps starry-eyed, is that since fictionists or literary-type writers are supposed to have some special interest in empathy, in trying to imagine what it's like to be the other guy, they might have some useful part to play in a political conversation that's having the problems ours is. Failing that, maybe at least we can help elevate some professional political journalists who are (1) polite, and (2) willing to entertain the possibility that intelligent,

well-meaning people can disagree, and (3) able to counte-
nance the fact that some problems are simply beyond the
ability of a single ideology to represent accurately.

Implicit in this brief, shrill answer, though, is obviously the idea that at least some political writing should be
Platonically disinterested, should rise above the fray, etc.;
and in my own present case this is impossible (and so I am
a hypocrite, an ideological opponent could say). In doing
the McCain piece you mentioned, I saw some stuff (more
accurately: I believe that I saw some stuff) about our current president, his inner circle, and the primary campaign
they ran that prompted certain reactions inside me that
make it impossible to rise above the fray. I am, at present,
partisan. Worse than that: I feel such deep, visceral antipa-
thy that I can't seem to think or speak or write in any kind
of fair or nuanced way about the current administration.
Writing-wise, I think this kind of interior state is dangerous.
It is when one feels most strongly, most personally, that
it's most tempting to speak up ("speak out" is the current
verb phrase of choice, rhetorically freighted as it is). But it's
also when it's the least productive, or at any rate it seems
that way to me—there are plenty of writers and journalists "speaking out" and writing pieces about oligarchy and
neofascism and mendacity and appalling short-sightedness
in definitions of "national security" and "national interest,"
etc., and very few of these writers seem to me to be generat-
ing helpful or powerful pieces, or really even being persua-
sive to anyone who doesn't already share the writer's views.

My own plan for the coming fourteen months is to

knock on doors and stuff envelopes. Maybe even to wear a button. To try to accrete with others into a demographically significant mass. To try extra hard to exercise patience, politeness, and imagination on those with whom I disagree. Also to floss more.

BLVR: Maybe that's a good segue into your work processes, which I guess I've begun to be fascinated with. If you want to talk about how, how often and where you write, I'm sure people would be interested.

DFW: Maybe you could talk briefly about your own work processes first. Why? (*a*) Because people'd be at least as interested in yours as mine. (*b*) Because you always have so much going on, both writing-wise and administration-wise. (*c*) So that I'd have a better idea of what you mean by "work processes."

BLVR: Right now I'm writing from a tiny library outside of San Francisco, in a carrel deep in their fiction stacks. I change my routine every four months or so, when my natural need to distract myself overcomes whatever routine-strategy I've been using to allow myself to work undistracted. This is my new thing, just begun last week and so far successful. After writing at home, in my brother's bedroom, for six months, now I go here. I have a small desk at 826 Valencia, but I can't do any actual writing there—it's in the middle of the office, so that's just for teaching, talking with staff and volunteers, meeting with people, etc. Given

the different things going on at McSwys/826, it gets hard—
as it does, I'm sure, for anyone who teaches—to carve out
the uninterrupted blocks of time you need to get quality
work done. I taught (high schoolers) last night until 9:30
p.m., and was supposed to teach (fifth graders) this morning at 10 a.m., and I had to give today's field trip to another
McSwys staffer/826 teacher, because I teach again tonight
and I was just feeling too squeezed, given that I've got four
deadlines this week. I'm a wuss, though. I'm sure there are
tons of writers who teach a hell of a lot more than I do. But
I guess like a lot of writers I need to isolate myself to the
degree that I can't use the phone or email or lawn mower or
bike, even if I need to—you have to distance yourself from
distractions.

Anyway, I remember you once actually answering your
phone by saying not "Hello" but "Distract me," which
struck me as the truest way to put it—when you pick up
the phone, you're leaving the submersion of good writerly
concentration. You've also said that you work on various
things concurrently. Can you talk about finding the time
you need, whether you write at night or by day, every day
or in binges, do you work on a PC/laptop/Commodore 64,
how often you teach, etc.?

DFW: I'm still not sure I've got much to relate. I know I
never work in whatever gets called an office, e.g., a school
office I use only for meeting students and storing books I
know I'm not going to read anytime soon. I know I used
to work mostly in restaurants, which chewing tobacco

rendered impractical in ways that are not hard to imagine. Then for a while I worked mostly in libraries. (By "working" I mean doing the first few drafts and revisions, which I do longhand. I've always typed at home, and I don't consider typing working, really.) Anyway, but then I started to have dogs. If you live by yourself and have dogs, things get strange. I know I'm not the only person who projects skewed parental neuroses onto his pets or companion-animals or whatever. But I have it pretty bad; it's a source of some amusement to friends. First, I began to get this strong feeling that it was traumatic for them to be left alone more than a couple hours. This is not quite as psycho as it may seem, because most of the dogs I've ended up with have had shall we say hard puppyhoods, including one past owner who went to jail. . . but that's neither here nor there. The point is that I got reluctant to leave them alone for very long, and then after a while I got so I actually needed one or more dogs around in order to be comfortable enough to feel like working. And all that put a crimp in outside-the-home writing, a change that in retrospect was not all that good for me because (*a*) I have agoraphobic tendencies anyway, and (*b*) home is obviously full of all kinds of distractions that library carrels aren't. The point being that I mostly work at home now, although I know I'd work better, faster, more concentratedly if I went someplace else. If work is going shitty, I try to make sure that at least a couple hours in the morning are carved out for this disciplined thing called Work. If it's going well, I often work in the p.m. too, although of course if it's going well it doesn't feel

disciplined or like uppercase Work because it's what I want
to be doing anyway. What often happens is that when work
goes well all my routines and disciplines go out the window
simply because I don't need them, and then when it starts
not going well I flounder around trying to reconstruct disciplines I can enforce and habits I can stick to. Which is
part of what I meant by saying that my way of doing it
seems chaotic, at least compared to the writing processes of
other people I know about (which now includes you).

BLVR: You said it better than I did. I should say that it
works the same way for me—a routine is just there for
when you're less inspired, or, in my case, when I'm trying to
do the last 7/8ths of something, which is always the tough-
est. But because you mentioned tobacco in your answer, I
want to ask about that. When I first met you, in New York
about five years ago, you were enjoying chewing tobacco at
a restaurant—that is, you had a dip-cup just beneath the
table, in which you deposited juice at a regular interval. Do
you want to talk about your history with various forms of
tobacco?

DFW: Let's acknowledge first that this Q actually preceded
the last one, and that you just inserted an artful little bridge-
sentence in your question-text to suggest otherwise. I know
you're interested in tobacco and the covert gradual suicide
that is habitual tobacco use. My own situation is not all that
different from Tom Bissell's, who had some article about
chewing tobacco in *Tumescent Male Monthly* or something

last year that I resonated with on many frequencies. I started smoking at twenty three after two years of dabbling in clove cigarettes (which were big in the early eighties). I liked cigarettes, very much, but one thing I did not like was how hard they were on the lungs and wind in terms of sports, stair-climbing, coitus, etc. Some roofer friends back home got me started on chew as a cigarette-substitute at I think age twenty eight. Chew doesn't hurt your lungs (obviously), but it also has massive, massive amounts of nicotine, at least compared to Marlboro Lights. (This, too, is all very condensed and boiled down; sorry if it's terse.) I have tried probably ten serious times to quit chewing tobacco in the last decade. I've never even made it a year. Besides all the well-documented psychic fallout, the hardest thing about quitting for me is that it makes me stupid. Really stupid. As in walking into rooms and forgetting why I'm there, drifting off in the middle of sentences, feeling coolness on my chin and discovering I've been drooling. Without chew, I have the attention span of a toddler. I giggle and sob inappropriately. And everything seems very, very far away. In essence it's like being unpleasantly stoned all the time. . . and as far as I can tell it's not a temporary withdrawal thing. I quit for eleven months once, and it was like that the whole time. On the other hand, chewing tobacco kills you—or at the very least it makes your teeth hurt and turn unpleasant colors and eventually fall out. Plus it's disgusting, and stupid, and a vector of self-contempt. So, once again, I've quit. It's now been a little over three months. At this moment I have in gum, a mint, and three Australian tea-tree

toothpicks that a Wiccan friend swears by. One reason you
and I are chatting in print rather than in real time is that
it's taken me twenty minutes just to formulate and press
the appropriate keys for the preceding ¶. Actually speaking
with me would be like visiting a demented person in a nurs-
ing home. Apparently I not only drift off in the middle of a
sentence but sometimes begin to hum, tunelessly, without
being aware of it. Also, FYI, my left eyelid has been twitch-
ing nonstop since August 18. It's not pretty. But I'd prefer to
live past fifty. This is my Tobacco Story.

BLVR: Another nice segue, about brains. [I say this while
pasting together the interview, which wasn't actually conducted in anything like the order it's now presented. But
I keep finding these nice segues, and wanted to share my
contentment with you, the *BLVR* reader.] You allude in
Everything and More to the fact that mathematicians have
taken on a somewhat sexy role in popular mythology, with
A Beautiful Mind, among other stories, helping to put
them in a place where, in the conventional wisdom, they
might even be supplanting artists as the presumed suffer-
ers of a sort of "mad genius" syndrome, the idea being that
they push the boundaries of their work so far that normal
life, and eventually their sanity, falls away. First, can you
comment on this assumption that to achieve, for example,
mathematical greatness, one might need to sacrifice his or
her sanity? (I realize that's a straw man.) Second, the G.K.
Chesterton quote you cite: "Poets do not go mad; but chess
players do..." echoes something my Evolution prof said at

U of Illinois (where your dad taught). He was talking about something called the homeostatic envelope, loosely defined (I think) as the limits of one's normal experience, from joy to depression—he drew a long rectangle and made a zig-zag lie-detector kind of line inside—with the ideal being that one would stay within this envelope, avoiding the lines exceeding it with too much joy or too much sadness. Anyway, the point he also made was that artists tend to stay more within the envelope, because of what I'm presuming he meant as the natural vents and releases built into their work, whereas the cashiers of the world might not have those. (Boy, I wonder if this makes any sense!) I guess I would ask whether you could comment on this vis-à-vis Chesterton's quote and the misperceptions about Cantor's own sanity or lack thereof, and also on your own mental journeys with your work. I tell my students that they should all try a novel at some point in their lives, given how irrevocably their mind will expand in the process. Having written an 1,100-page novel and now *Everything and More*, can you talk about your own brain-expansion/self-discovery/forays into temporary "madness"?

DFW: Well, hmm. I think what I'll do is spell out the very specific contexts in which the madness-v.-genius thing gets mentioned in the book. It may be too specific to provide the sort of answer your question seems to invite. The real answer's too heavy to get into generally in this sort of context, even if I had the equipment for it. (I suspect what I'd do in a general discussion is spray a lot of verbiage and finally end up saying I don't think anybody's ever really improved on Nietzsche's stuff about the Apollo-Dionysus interplay as a way to conceive both the madness-v.-genius thing and our Western fascination with it.)

There are two reasons for mentioning the genius-v.-madness stuff at the start of *E&M*. One is to introduce the idea of abstractness as both a feature of math and an engine of neurosis, which intro then enables §1's whole long thing on just what abstraction is and why it's so important to talking about math. I can't recall whether it got cut during any of the book's myriad editorial snafus and reworkings, but at one point there was a short, 100% true bit in like §5 about math's symbolism being so intimidating to most people not because it's hard to understand per se (which it really isn't) but because it's such a perfectly abstract compression of massive amounts of information. Anyway. . .

The other reason calls for some tact on my part. It so happens that just as initial work for *E&M* got underway, a certain book came out, a pop bio of Cantor by a certain author whom I won't name except to say that his initials are the same as those of a well-known commercial airline. For a certain publisher whose own name sounds like an autistic person's description of a room. This unnamed book had two main theses about Cantor's work on ∞: one was that it was intimately bound up with mystical Judaism and the metaphysics of the kabala; the other was that ∞ was such a mind-blowing math concept that grappling with it drove Cantor mad, which madness's symptoms, hospitalizations, etc. then got detailed and lingered over with all kinds of

anecdotes and photos. The kabala stuff was mildly interesting, although there wasn't much in the way of actual
argument for any of the connections the book alleged. But
the ∞-drove-Cantor-mad stuff was dreck, the very worst
kind of appeal to a flabby, unconsidered pop version of
what you just now called the "'mad genius' syndrome." The
origin, motives, and contexts of Cantor's actual achievement got little serious treatment in this unnamed book,
basically I think because airline-initials and/or autistic-
room-description felt the math would be too dull for a
mainstream audience. What math there is in that book is
sexed up by making it seem like ∞ was some transcendent
forbidden terrain that Cantor lost his mind trying to nego-
tiate. Whereas the fact is that it's all but certain that Cantor
was bipolar, that his professional insecurities and travails
aggravated the illness but didn't cause it, that most of his
worst episodes and hospitalizations occurred when he was
older and his best work was long behind him. Etc., etc.—
some of the unsexy truth gets talked about in *E&M*. What
was most irksome to me about this unnamed prior book,
though, was the author's/publisher's apparent assumption
that Cantor's theories themselves were not beautiful or accessible or important enough in their own right to base a
general-interest book around (which in fact they are), and
thus that the math of ∞ had to be recast as some kind of
intellectual Lost Ark that made Cantor's face melt off when
he looked inside it. I hope I'm still being tactful. The truth
is that this unnamed book really bugged me: It managed at
once to insult Cantor and his work, the reader, and the very

possibility of writing honestly about technical stuff for a general audience. Anyway, to the limited extent that *E&M* does mention the "mad genius" thing, just about all these mentions are meant to be direct, emphatic replies to this unidentified prior book.

BLVR: According to one of the more science-oriented people at the *Believer,* there is a wave of new "pop" math books. Which ones do you think are worthwhile? Do you like *Flatland*? *Gödel, Escher, Bach*? I think you've mentioned that you like *A Mathematician's Apology*. . .

DFW: It depends, of course, what you mean by "pop." Hardy's *Apology* is pop in the sense of being totally accessible to anybody with a twelfth-grade vocabulary, but it's not pop in that only people with enough of a math background to give a bright blue fart about the psychology and aesthetics of pure math will care very much about the book's subject. So hmmm. *G, E, B* is a great book, but it's hard: I personally don't think Hofstadter does enough teaching of the basic concepts to make his riffs and dialogues come alive for people who didn't have a lot of basic logic and recursion-theory in college (I actually shoved this book excitedly at people in the eighties who thought it was a drag; it turned out they didn't have the prep.) And so on. Your science guy would have to ask me on a book-by-book basis, almost. In general, things that sell really well, e.g. Aczel's, are usually dreck. Actually, most Four Walls Eight Windows pop tech stuff sucks; what they seem really good at is marketing their dreck. But not all major-house stuff is bad. Seife's book about zero for Viking a few years ago was surprisingly good, although it was also accessible as hell. In general, I think the whole pop-math genre is confused and confusing because nobody's exactly sure who the audience is or how to pitch the discussion.

BLVR: Here's a big, broad-implication type of question from Gideon (Lewis-Kraus), a copyeditor and assistant editor here: You note that throughout mathematical (and, by extension, mathematico-philosophical or philo-mathematical or whatever) history, the concept of infinity was regarded as not just elusive & confusing & confounding in terms of various mathematical taxonomies, but downright dangerous: The closest thing that the Greeks had to a concept of infinity was essentially the idea of messiness, of chaotic Dionysian disorganization. So infinity challenged their rigorously maintained ideas of logical law & order, etc.; the Christians and the Scholastics feared the concept of infinity in mathematics because it somehow defied the omnipotence & uniqueness of the one God. But then, when we finally get this workable, interesting, courageous attempt to understand and define the concept of infinity in the latter half of the nineteenth century, the concept that falls out is fascinating and clever and mathematically revolutionary and really a tremendous poetic achievement, but, as far as I can tell, it hasn't had much relevance outside of a narrowly circumscribed math world, and hasn't been particularly dangerous, or, if it has been relevant and/or dangerous, you don't really go into what any of the extra-mathematical implications have been. Is there anything to say on this subject? Are there interesting infinity-related extra-mathematical implications of Cantor and his discoveries?

DFW: Probably the quickest, most efficient way to respond is to say that this question leads nicely into the whole reason why pop-tech books might have some kind of special utility in today's culture. The big difference is that things are vastly more compartmentalized now than they were up through, say, the Renaissance. And more specialized, and more freighted with all kinds of special context. There's no way we'd expect a world-class, cutting-edge mathematician now also to be doing world-class, cutting-edge philosophy, theology, etc. Not so for the Greeks—if only because math, philosophy, and theology weren't coherently distinguishable for them. Same for the Neoplatonists and Scholastics, and etc. etc. (This is a very, very simple answer, of course, maybe right on the edge of simplistic.) By the time Cantor weighed in on ∞ in the 1870s, it was part of an extremely specialized technical discipline that took decades to master and be able to do advanced work in. For Cantor and R. Dedekind (and now this is all just condensed way down from the book (sort of the same way the question is)), the math of ∞ is derived as a way to solve certain thorny problems in post-calc analysis (viz., the expansions of trig functions and the rigorous definition of irrational numbers, respectively), which problems themselves derive from K. Weierstrass's solutions to certain earlier problems, and so on. It's all so abstract and specialized that large parts of *E&M* end up getting devoted to unpacking the problems clearly enough so that a general reader can get a halfway realistic idea of where set theory and the topology of the Real Line even come from, mathematically speaking. The real point, I think, has to do with something else that ends up mentioned only quickly in the book's final draft. We live today in a world where most of the really important developments in everything from math and physics and astronomy to public policy and psychology and classical music are so extremely abstract and technically complex and context-dependent that it's next to impossible for the ordinary citizen to feel that they (the developments) have much relevance to her actual life. Where even people in two closely related sub-sub-specialties have a hard time communicating with each other because their respective s-s-s's require so much special training and knowledge. And so on. Which is one reason why pop-technical writing might have value (beyond just a regular book-market $-value), as part of the larger frontier of clear, lucid, unpatronizing technical communication. It might be that one of the really significant problems of today's culture involves finding ways for educated people to talk meaningfully with one another across the divides of radical specialization. That sounds a bit gooey, but I think there's some truth to it. And it's not just the polymer chemist talking to the semiotician, but people with special expertise acquiring the ability to talk meaningfully to us, meaning ordinary schmoes. Practical examples: Think of the thrill of finding a smart, competent

IT technician who can also explain what she's doing in such a way that you feel like you understand what went wrong with your computer and how you might even fix the problem yourself if it comes up again. Or an oncologist who can communicate clearly and humanly with you and your wife about what the available treatments for her stage-two neoplasm are, and about how the different treatments actually work, and exactly what the plusses and minuses of each one are. If you're like me, you practically drop and hug the ankles of technical specialists like this, when you find them. As of now, of course, they're rare. What they have is a particular kind of genius that's not really part of their specific area of expertise as such areas are usually defined and taught. There's not really even a good univocal word for this kind of genius—which might be significant. Maybe there should be a word; maybe being able to communicate with people outside one's area of expertise should be taught, and talked about, and considered as a requirement for genuine expertise... Anyway, that's the sort of stuff I think your question is nibbling at the edges of, and it's interesting as hell.

BLVR: I'm just noticing that we didn't get to talk about your teaching much. I've met a few students who attended Pomona in large part because you were teaching there. What's the title of your class? What's on your reading list? Do you use chalk or wipe-away markers?

DFW: Packed into this Q is the idea that what I'm really talking about w/r/t people communicating with each other across specialties is people becoming better teachers, which I'm not sure whether I was saying that or not. Teaching is different, I think, since the students are there voluntarily, and are by definition young and labile and pre-specialized. Anyway, I know that's not what you're asking. I have a lottery-prize-type gig at Pomona: The formal duties are light, the students all have way better SAT scores than I did, and I get to do more or less what I want. I'm doing Intro Fiction right now, which is fun because it's a chance to take kids who are very experienced in literary criticism and paper-writing and to show them there's a totally—in some ways diametrically—different way to read and write. Which would all take a long time to talk about, but for the most part it's big fun, and now that I don't stop and spit brownly into a coffee can every two minutes my credibility with the kids has gone way up; and as long as I don't do something really egregious I think I get to stay as long as I want.

"SOME KIND OF TERRIBLE BURDEN"

INTERVIEW BY STEVE PAULSON

FIRST BROADCAST ON *TO THE BEST OF OUR KNOWLEDGE*

JUNE 17, 2004

PAULSON: I'm speaking with David Foster Wallace, whose new collection of stories is called *Oblivion*. I want to start by talking about one particular story, "The Soul Is Not a Smithy." How would you describe this story?

WALLACE: As longer than I intended it to be? A little kid with attention problems in school is not attending on a very dramatic day for him where his teacher kind of has a psychotic breakdown.

PAULSON: His substitute teacher starts writing "Kill Them" over and over on the blackboard, and then when these kids in the fourth grade start realizing what he's doing, that he's basically lost his marbles, they panic.

WALLACE: Yes.

PAULSON: But your narrator who is reflecting back on that time, his mind was actually elsewhere because he had been staring out the window watching other strange stuff.

WALLACE: Yeah, it's weird because the narrator is partly narrating as a child and partly as an adult. But mainly his

big concern is how boring and meaningless his life has been
and how he's missed the one really dramatic thing that ever
happened to him. It's actually more interesting than that—
I'm not making it sound very...

PAULSON: It's actually a fascinating story, and I think fascinating partly because it takes a turn somewhere else, really
near the end, and it becomes kind of about a child's fear
of the adult world and what seems to be this boy's fear of
becoming like his own father, who is an insurance actuary.
I'm wondering if you could read a passage from the story,
I'm thinking maybe starting around page 103 or so.

WALLACE: No, I understand. So I should start now?

PAULSON: Yes.

[Wallace reads a passage from The Soul is Not a Smithy
beginning "For my own Part..." and ending "... dreamed
in the real world."]

PAULSON: That's wonderful, thank you. So evocative. You
know I have to say that when I first read that passage it
seemed like something right out of Kafka, sort of the night-
mare quality of the ordinary world. Does that have any
resonance for you?

WALLACE: Well, no, it's a weird story because the story
started out really surreal and then parts of this are actually

the climax, but the climax is much more sort of plain, ev-
eryday realistic than surreal, so it ended up kind of like
inverted Kafka for me. It's a very strange, very strange piece,
I think.

PAULSON: Did you have that kind of dread when you were
a kid?

WALLACE: I think, I think in a country where we have it as
easy as we do, one of our big dread vectors is boredom, and
I think little edges of despair and soul-level boredom appear
in things like homework or particularly dry classroom stuff.
I can remember the incredible soaring relief of when certain
teachers would say we were going to watch a movie in grade
school. And it wasn't just a hedonistic "Oh, we're going to
have fun." It was a relief from some kind of terrible burden,
I thought. So, I don't know. Maybe.

PAULSON: Did you look at what your parents were doing,
your father, in particular, and think, "Oh my god, I don't
want to become like that"?

WALLACE: I don't know, both my parents were teachers so
they always got pale and haunted looking when there were
big stacks of papers to grade. But I think a lot of this has
more to do with, with friends' parents, and friends who
have become kind of office workers. I just got interested in
the reality of boredom, which is something that I think is
a hugely important problem and yet none of us talk about

it because we all act like it's just sort of something that we have to get through, which I suppose we do.

PAULSON: Well it's funny because as I was reading that I was thinking back to my own childhood, and my father was a professor and he would—after dinner he would typically go on up to his study and close the door and—I don't know what he did. But I remember thinking when I was petty little that this doesn't seem like fun to have to do this, night after night, and I didn't want to become like that. Of course, I sort of have become like that because I go home, and I have my own homework as well. But I'm wondering if that resonated at all for you?

WALLACE: One of my little family stories that Mom always tells is that on the day in second grade when we all had to talk about what our fathers did for a living, I said my father didn't do anything for a living, he just stayed home and wrote on yellow paper. Because he was a professor, too. I know that part of what interested me in this story was trying to remember what I thought about what my parents did when I was a child. Because when you're a child I don't think you're aware of how incredibly easy you have it, right? You have your own problems and you have your own burdens and chores and things you have to do, but, yeah, I think my intuitions were very much like yours. I think when they went into these quiet rooms and had to do things that it wasn't obvious they wanted to do, I think there was a part of me that felt that something terrible was coming. But also, of course, now that we're putatively grown up there's also a lot of really, really interesting stuff and sometimes you sit in quiet rooms and do a lot of drudgery and at the end of it is a surprise or something very rewarding or a feeling of fulfillment.

PAULSON: That's the life of a writer, isn't it?

WALLACE: Yeah, but it's also probably the life of a radio-host, and probably, in many cases, the life of office workers, who—who we think of as having very boring, dry jobs. Probably all jobs are the same and they're filled with horrible boredom and despair and quiet little bits of fulfillment that are very hard to tell anyone else about. That's just a guess.

PAULSON: You know what I find interesting about what we've been talking about, and also the passage you've just read is: your public image as a writer: you're typically described as one of the leading figures of the postmodern hip ironic generation of writers in their thirties and early forties, but I read somewhere that you really think of yourself as a realist.

WALLACE: Well, except, you know. . . These various classifications are important for critics, right? You have to form different things into groups or else you have to talk about a trillion different particulars. I don't know very many writers who don't think of themselves as realists, in terms of trying to convey the way stuff tastes and feels to you. This is a good example of a story where... I mean, a lot of stuff that's capital-R Realism just seems to me somewhat hokey, because obviously realism is an illusion of realism, and the idea that small banal details are somehow more real or authentic than large or strange details always seemed to me to be just a little bit crude. But this was an interesting piece to write because during the real payoff part of it it did become extremely realistic and small and filled with banal details. The truth of the matter is that when you're in an interview you have to say all kinds of stuff; I don't really know what I am and I don't think very many writers have any idea what they are. You just try to do stuff that feels alive to you.

PAULSON: I'm wondering, particularly for people of our generation—I think we're roughly around the same age, we're both in our early forties—whether there's a certain cultural landscape that you feel most compelled to write about.

WALLACE: I know that when I was in graduate school those of us who wrote very much about what used to be called pop culture or advertising or television were really—were really scorned by our older professors, who saw that stuff as kind of vapid and banal, and lacking a kind of Platonic timelessness. And I remember it was a really big source of conflict because in lots of ways we just didn't get what they were saying. I mean, this was our world and our reality, the same way, you know, the Romantics' world was trees and babbling brooks and mountains and blue skies. So, I think probably if there's—yeah, I'm forty-two, and if there's something that's distinctive about our generation it's that we've been steeped in media and marketing since the time we were very, very small. And it's kind of a grand experiment because no other generation in the history of the world has been that mediated. What implications that has, I don't know, but I know it affects what seems urgent and worth writing about and what kind of feels real in my head when I'm working on it.

PAULSON: Isn't that also complicated, though, because the danger of writing about what you'd call mass culture or pop culture is that it's going to seem shallow. In fact, you wrote an essay about this some years back, about the risk of just being clever, and I guess it's—how do you say something original about this world that in so many ways is really pretty shallow?

WALLACE: The way to answer is with a platitude, but some platitudes are kind of deep. For me, art that's alive and urgent is art that's about what it is to be a human being. And whether one is a human being in times of enormous profundity and depth and challenge, or one is trying to be a human being in times of what appears to be shallow and commercial and materialistic, really isn't all that relevant to the deeper picture—I'm sorry, to the deeper project. The deeper project is: what is it to be human? There are certain paradoxes and there are certain hazards involved in writing about this world because a lot of commercial culture is itself based on kinds of art, at least sort of pop art, and it can get... there's the danger of being sucked into it, and simply trying, for instance, to do something that seems very hip and clever and thinking the job has been done then. I've certainly done stuff like that, and realized only later with horror that what I did was, in fact, just regurgitated the same stuff that I've been hearing since I was four or five. There's another side to it, though, I think, that part of this division in postmodern experimentalists and realists is—at least for people like me, I'm forty-two and I grew up, I don't know how many afterschool specials and Hallmark network things I've seen—a lot of what is quote unquote Realistic—conventionally Realistic—ends up seeming hokey to me. The resolutions seem contrived, everything seems a little bit too convenient and platitudish, and the ultimate goal of it is to sell me something. And there's a part of me, I think, that recoils from that, and that's a problem because some Realistic stuff really is alive and urgent, but the model and the form has been so exhaustively mined for commercial reasons that I think for a lot of us about our age, we're looking for different, less commercial forms in which to talk about the urgent, moving stuff. I don't know whether that makes any sense, but that's pretty much the truth the way I see it.

PAULSON: I think the other piece of that is a lot of this commercial world, whether it's movies or advertising even, it's pretty compelling, it's entertaining—and I suppose, from a writer's perspective, you might feel that if you want to write about this stuff, you have to be entertaining, too.

WALLACE: Yeah, well, there's that danger; the other danger is, to reprise an early twentieth-century painting thing, where once there was photography the interest in mimesis in painting really disappeared and everything got really abstract—it's a real problem. I don't have a TV anymore, but when I'm doing something like this and I'm on the road I watch TV in hotels and I'm appalled by how good the commercials have gotten. They're fascinating, they're funny, they're hip, they've got trunk lines into my high-school level anxieties and desires in a way that the commercials I grew up with never did. What it is, is a lot of them are the hip, cynical, cool people I went to college feeling intimidated by, who are now making two million dollars a year, figuring out how to do this stuff. And they've gotten very, very good at it.

PAULSON: I have to ask you about another of your stories, "The Suffering Channel," which among other things deals with a new kind of reality TV show that shows real-life episodes of torture and murder and rape and all of that. Is that sort of your vision of what might happen in some dystopian future?

WALLACE: I don't know that it's that, I think, to the extent that I understand reality TV, it has a certain logic, and it's not hard to take that logic to its extreme. I think celebrity autopsy, while childhood friends of the celebrity sit around

talking about whether or not this celebrity was a good person while his or her organs are being excised would be kind
of the terminus of that logic. But the question is how far
we go. The inhibition of shame on the part both of the
contestants and on the part of the people who put together
the show—at some point people have figured out that even
if viewers are sneering or talking about in what poor taste
stuff is, they're still watching, and that they key is to get
people to watch, and that that's what's remunerative. And
I think that once we lost that shame hobble, only time will
tell how far we'll go.

PAULSON: Your essays and your fiction are famous for various things—for their footnotes, for various digressions on
all kinds of sort of odd bits of information, obscure bits of
science and philosophy. Are you just drawn to this kind of
thing, do you just have a hunger to know about the world?

WALLACE: I don't know if it's that so much as, you know,
a lot of it really does come back to trying to do something
that feels real to me. And—I don't really know what the interior of anybody else is like—I often feel very fragmented,
and as if I have a symphony of different voices, and voice-
overs, and factoids, going on all the time and digressions
on digressions on digressions, and I know that people who
don't much care for my stuff see a lot of the stuff as just sort
of vomiting it out. That's at least my intent, what's hard
is to seem very digressive and bent in on yourself and dif-
fracted and yet also have there be patterns and significances

about it, and it takes a lot of drafts, but it probably comes out just looking like, you know, a manic mad monologue or something. I don't know that I'm more interested in trivia or factoids than anybody else—I know that they sort of bounce around in my head an awful lot.

PAULSON: I came across a quote from the novelist Zadie Smith, who said, "It's not the writer's job to tell us how somebody felt about something, it's to tell us how the world works." Do you agree with that?

WALLACE: Well, what you've got there is a very clever statement on one side of this division between capital-R Realism and something more experimental or postmodern with a kind of social agenda. Probably if you backed me into a tight corner what I'd say is ultimately there's no difference between those two things, although they're different as philosophies via which to proceed in the project. But if you could articulate—if you could articulate well enough what something felt like to somebody, you would have a fantastic template for how the world worked. That might be a kind of solipsistic view, but I sort of think it's mine. But also, Zadie is very clever and what she calls a wind-up merchant, and I think part of her saying that is just to get people revved up.

PAULSON: But you're also suggesting that it's sort of the way science is going, that as the study of consciousness gets—I don't know—more and more complicated, to some degree it's all in our mind anyway, I mean, how we perceive the world, so maybe there really isn't this distinction between the world out there and how we make sense of it in our own minds.

WALLACE: Yeah, but the other tricky thing is that the only way we can talk to each other about this is with language, and in language, built in is the idea of this distinction you just presented to me, so maybe there is nothing outside the mind. If there is nothing outside the mind, it's really not a very big deal that there isn't. But when we talk to each other about it, there automatically becomes a big deal. So, language, and the way we have to communicate with each other and process the world through words I think is the wild card in all this, and I don't totally understand it, but. . . So the answer just kind of tails off, I'm afraid.

PAULSON: You were a philosophy student at one point, weren't you?

WALLACE: I was.

PAULSON: Does that impulse still stay with you?

WALLACE: Oh, I think at the time that I was studying philosophy it was the beginning of the infiltration by kind of continental deconstruction on analytic philosophy and the world was full of recursion, and involution, and things bending back on themselves, and various incarnations of

Gödel's proof, and I think some of that kind of affected me at a spinal level. I really like recursions, and I really like contradictions and paradoxes and statements that kind of negate themselves in the middle. But I think at this point in my life it seems to me to be more of a tic than anything really all that important.

PAULSON: I mentioned this essay that you wrote, I think it was back in 1993, about writing and sort of what various fiction writers are up to, and one point you made is that irony tyrannizes us. The implicit message of irony is, "I don't really mean what I'm saying," and you went on to suggest that the next generation of rebel writers might ditch irony in favor of sincerity, I think I'm quoting here, "who treat plain old untrendy human troubles and emotions with reverence and conviction. Who eschew self-consciousness and hip fatigue."

WALLACE: Yeah?

PAULSON: Is that a critique of your own kind of writing?

WALLACE: I don't know that it's that. The thing even sounds dated to me now. I think it's less that than an articulation of the thing you were asking me about before: you know, what is it like to be working really hard on this stuff at age forty-two having been marketed to all your life. And, uh, how does one... Because you want your art to be hip and seem cool to people, you want people to like the stuff, but a great

deal of what passes for hip or cool is now highly, highly com-
mercially driven. And some of it I think is important art. I
think *The Simpsons* is important art. On the other hand, it's
also, in my opinion, relentlessly corrosive to the soul, and
everything is parodied, and everything is ridiculous. And,
maybe I'm old, but for my part I can be steeped in about
an hour of it, and then I sort of have to walk away and look
at a flower or something. If there's something to be talked
about, that thing is this weird conflict between what my
girlfriend calls the "inner sap", you know? The part of us
that can really wholeheartedly weep at stuff, and the part of
us that has to live in a world of smart, jaded, sophisticated
people and wants very much to be taken seriously by those
people. I don't know that it's that irony tyrannizes us, but
the fashions that are so easy to criticize but are so incredibly
powerful and authentic-seeming when we're inside them,
tyrannize us. I don't know that it's ever been any different.
That probably makes absolutely no sense.

PAULSON: No, actually it makes total—

WALLACE: That was my experiment at telling the truth.

PAULSON: It makes total sense. But can you hold those two
impulses simultaneously?

WALLACE: No, but I think my personal opinion—and
what I tell my students—is that if there's suffering involved
in art, or however you want to say it, right now this is the

form of the suffering: is to be the battleground for the war between those two kind of impulses. Neither of which are stupid, neither of which are wrong, but it's not at all clear to me how to marry them. And I don't think it's been at all clear since about the 1950s. And I just think it's where we're at.

PAULSON: Is that what you're trying to do in your fiction— to sort of get at those two impulses within the same work, the same story?

WALLACE: For the purposes of this conversation I'll say yes, but sitting in a bright, quiet room in front of the paper it's much more: uhh does this make me want to throw up? Does this seem real? Is this the sort of thing the person would say? It's much more kind of boneheaded and practical than that. You realize this, right? There's something very artificial about once the book's all through galleys and, you know, now I'm engaging in critical discourse about it—I might be right, but it's very different than what it's like actually to do the things.

PAULSON: Sure, that makes total sense.

WALLACE: The stuff that's in my mind as I'm doing it is far less sophisticated than this.

PAULSON: There's one last thing I'd love to ask you about, if you're willing. I'm doing a story for NPR about Dale Peck, who I'm sure is not your favorite critic. Um, could I ask you a couple questions about him?

WALLACE: Yeah, but why would you assume he's not my favorite critic?

PAULSON: Because he's written nasty stuff about your work. Maybe I'm presuming too much—have you read his writing about your writing?

WALLACE: Not about—I don't read reviews of my own stuff. I read a James Atlas piece in the *New York Times Magazine* about Dale Peck and the *New Republic* and that whole strategy so I know generally what you're talking about, but uh, yeah, OK. I mean, no, I'll play, I don't have a personal—I haven't read the stuff so I don't have a personal pissing contest thing with him.

PAULSON: Yeah, OK.

WALLACE: Well, that can be edited out.

PAULSON: As you've probably heard he's very critical of I guess a cluster of writers who've typically been lumped together: you and Rick Moody, and other people who usually fall under the rubric of the postmodern descendants of Thomas Pynchon. I mean I'm wildly generalizing of course, and, um, he was particularly very critical of *Infinite Jest*. Do you—

WALLACE: He was not alone, by the way.

PAULSON: Do you feel any need to sort of—when you see a broadside like that, do you want to respond?

WALLACE: No, well the thing about reviews... Number one, reading a review of your own stuff is like listening—if you had a chance to overhear two people talking about you, right? You'd do it, but you wouldn't be glad you did it, because the conversation's not for you, and it always ends up making you crazy and hurting your feelings. So, after having been at this a while, I just no longer read them. I think book reviewing is a hard business. I've done some book reviews, it's difficult to do. In my opinion it's far more difficult to write a review of something that you don't like because if you're a fiction writer you know how hard you work even on something that seems really crummy to somebody else. I think it's possible sometimes to accuse certain critics of being mostly interested in their own reputation for being kind of a hardass or for making waves, and any time you've got a book review whose main agenda is to advance the reputation of the book critic, I think people ought to run for cover, because it's very very very different from whatever that enterprise is supposed to be, which is basically a good-faith attempt to talk to civilians about whether they might want to spend money or time on something.

PAULSON: Yeah, and I think what's surprised a lot of people about Dale Peck's criticism is that considering that he himself is a novelist, he seems awfully savage, and I mean to put it bluntly he said of *Infinite Jest* that eight hundred pages of it was crap.

WALLACE: Well, let me just point out... Y'know what? And I don't have any kind of response to that, but I would just say, remember when we talked about once the shame hobble is off? All you gotta do is say something really really inflammatory and then people are talking about you, y'know? And if you're the sort of person who doesn't mind that a lot of what people say is kind of horrified or appalled or controversial, then you're set. If what you want to do is be talked about, really it's all you gotta do. I don't know Dale Peck, I don't know what his agenda is, I know that a lot of this sort of in-your-face trash-talking review stuff is in certain ways very cunning, because it creates a lot of attention, for the reviewer and the review, and maybe in an ancillary way for the book. Maybe somebody goes out and says, Oh, what is all this crap, I mean, I don't like this reviewer so maybe I'll go get this thing. Who knows? The whole thing seems about as interesting to me as a high-school cat-fight. But considerably more profitable.

PAULSON: Do you do much... I guess I don't really see much reviewing that you do of other works of fiction. Is that something that you pretty much just want to stay away from?

WALLACE: I did some in the late eighties, mainly just

because I was really poor. That's another thing people don't know is, these are hard and you don't get paid that much to do them. You're often in a bad mood when you do them. I do, I mean I do sort of long reviewish things that then turn into essays because I'm in the luxurious position of being able to do that, but week in week out month in month out book reviewing is a tough business, and I'd be very hesitant to make any judgments of anybody who's doing it. Having just implicitly done that of Dale Peck, of course. But really, if you run any of that, you've gotta say, except for hearing about what he said about Moody's thing in that *Atlas* article, I don't know anything about the guy. I was on a panel with him once. I remember he wore leather pants and I found it unusual. And that was my one impression of Dale Peck. More power to him, as far as I'm concerned. I just feel like he and I are just not even in the same area code. And anybody who's reading his reviews of my stuff, seriously, is probably not gonna be interested in my stuff anyway. So what difference does it make?

THE LAST
INTERVIEW

INTERVIEW BY CHRISTOPHER FARLEY

FIRST PUBLISHED IN THE *WALL STREET JOURNAL*

MAY 2008

David Foster Wallace, author of the novel *Infinite Jest*, was asked by *Rolling Stone* magazine to cover John McCain's presidential campaign in 2000. That assignment became a chapter in his essay collection *Consider the Lobster* (2005); the essay has now been issued as a stand-alone book, *McCain's Promise*. In a phone interview, Mr. Wallace said he came away from the experience marveling at "how unknowable and layered these candidates are." Mr. Wallace also answered questions via email about presidential hopefuls, the youth vote and smiley faces.

WSJ: So why would a novelist want to travel around on a campaign bus?

MR. WALLACE: What made the McCain idea interesting to me, was that I'd seen a tape of his appearance on Charlie Rose at some point the previous year, in which he spoke so candidly and bluntly about stuff like campaign finance and partisan ickiness, stuff I'd not heard any national-level politician say. There was also the fact that my own politics were about 179 degrees from his, so there was no worry that I'd somehow get seduced into writing an infomercial.

WSJ: Have you changed your mind about any of the points that you made in the book?

MR. WALLACE: In the best political tradition, I reject the premise of your question. The essay quite specifically concerns a couple weeks in February, 2000, and the situation of both McCain [and] national politics in those couple weeks. It is heavily context-dependent. And that context now seems a long, long, long time ago. McCain himself has obviously changed; his flipperoos and weaselings on Roe v. Wade, campaign finance, the toxicity of lobbyists, Iraq timetables, etc. are just some of what make him a less interesting, more depressing political figure now—for me, at least. It's all understandable, of course—he's the GOP nominee now, not an insurgent maverick. Understandable, but depressing. As part of the essay talks about, there's an enormous difference between running an insurgent Hail-Mary-type longshot campaign and being a viable candidate (it was right around New Hampshire in 2000 that McCain began to change from the former to the latter), and there are some deep, really rather troubling questions about whether serious honor and candor and principle remain possible for someone who wants to really maybe win. I wouldn't take back anything that got said in that essay, but I'd want a reader to keep the time and context very much in mind on every page.

WSJ: You write that John McCain, in 2000, had become "the great populist hope of American politics." What parallels do you see between McCain in 2000 and Barack Obama in 2008?

MR. WALLACE: There are some similarities—the ability to attract new voters, Independents; the ability to raise serious money in a grassroots way via the Web. But there are also lots of differences, many too obvious to need pointing out. Obama is an orator, for one thing—a rhetorician of the old school. To me, that seems more classically populist than McCain, who's not a good speechmaker and whose great strengths are Q&As and small-group press confabs. But there's a bigger [reason]. The truth—as I see it—is that the previous seven years and four months of the Bush Administration have been such an unmitigated horror show of rapacity, hubris, incompetence, mendacity, corruption, cynicism and contempt for the electorate that it's very difficult to imagine how a self-identified Republican could try to position himself as a populist.

WSJ: In the book, you talk about why many young people are turned off by politics. What do you think could get young people to the voting booth this election?

MR. WALLACE: Well, it's a very different situation. If nothing else, the previous seven years and four months have helped make it clear that it actually matters a whole, whole lot who gets elected president. A whole lot. There's also the fact that there are now certain really urgent, galvanizing problems—price of oil, carbon emissions, Iraq—that are apt to get more voters of all ages and education-levels to the polls. For more interested or sophisticated young voters, there are also the matters of the staggering rise in national debt and off-the-books war-funding, the collapse of the dollar, and the grievous damage that's been done to all manner of consensuses about Constitutional protections, separation of powers, and US obligations under international treaties.

WSJ: You're known for writing big, complex books. Your novel *Infinite Jest* is more than 1,000 pages, but *McCain's Promise* is a trim 124 pages. What made you decide to drop a few weight classes for this release?

MR. WALLACE: The truth is that this book is really a magazine article whose subject just turned out to be too big and thorny and multiramified to be doable at article length.

WSJ: I have an advance copy of Infinite Jest that your publishing house sent me in 1996. It's signed—apparently—by you and there's a little smiley face under your name. I've always wondered—did you actually draw that smiley face?

MR WALLACE: One prong of the Buzz plan [for *Infinite Jest*] involved sending out a great many signed first editions—or maybe reader copies—to people who might generate Buzz. What they did was mail me a huge box of trade-paperback-size sheets of paper, which I was to sign; they would then somehow stitch them in to these "special" books. I basically spent an entire weekend signing these pages. You've probably had the weird epileptoid experience of saying a word over and over until it ceases to denote and becomes very strange and arbitrary and odd-feeling—imagine that happening with your own name. That's what happened. Plus it was boring. So boring, that I started doing all kinds of weird little graphic things to try to stay alert and engaged. What you call the "smiley face" is a vestige of an amateur cartoon character I used to amuse myself with in grade school. It's physically fun to draw—very sharp and swooping, and the eyebrows are just crackling with affect. I've seen a few of these "special books" at signings before, and it always makes me smile to see that face.

DAVID FOSTER WALLACE (1962–2008) was an American novelist, short-story writer and essayist. He is best known for his thousand-page novel *Infinite Jest*, published in 1996. He also wrote the short-story collections *Girl with Curious Hair*, *Brief Interviews with Hideous Men* and *Oblivion*, and nonfiction for, among others, *Harper's*, *Rolling Stone*, *The Atlantic Monthly* and *TENNIS Magazine*. Collected editions of his nonfiction include *Consider the Lobster* and *A Supposedly Fun Thing I'll Never Do Again*. He was widely hailed as the voice of a generation and won numerous awards and fellowships, and his unfinished novel *The Pale King*, published posthumously in 2011, was nominated for the Pulitzer Prize. In the years before his death Wallace taught at Pomona College in California.

LAURA MILLER is a co-founder of Salon.com and writes for the *New York Times Book Review*, the *New Yorker*, the *Los Angeles Times* and the *Wall Street Journal*. She is the author of *The Magician's Book: A Skeptic's Adventures in Narnia*.

TOM SCOCCA is the managing editor of *Deadspin* and the author of *Beijing Welcomes You: Unveiling the Capital City of the Future*.

STACEY SCHMEIDEL works in college public relations and is a free-lance writer.

DAVE EGGERS is an award-winning American writer, editor and publisher. His books include *A Heartbreaking Work of Staggering Genius*, *What is the What* and *Zeitoun*. He is the founder and editor of the independent publishing house McSweeney's.

STEVE PAULSON is the Executive Producer and a co-founder of *To the Best of Our Knowledge*. He has been a contributing writer for *Salon* and has written for *Slate*, *the Huffington Post* and other publications. He is the author of *Atoms and Eden: Conversations on Religion and Science*.

CHRISTOPHER FARLEY is the editor of Speakeasy, the *Wall Street Journal*'s culture website. He's worked as a senior special writer at the *Wall Street Journal* and as a senior editor at the *Weekend Wall Street Journal*.

THE LAST INTERVIEW SERIES

KURT VONNEGUT: THE LAST INTERVIEW

"I think it can be tremendously refreshing if a creator of literature has something on his mind other than the history of literature so far. Literature should not disappear up its own asshole, so to speak."

$15.95 / $17.95 CAN
978-1-61219-090-7
ebook: 978-1-61219-091-4

LEARNING TO LIVE FINALLY: THE LAST INTERVIEW
JACQUES DERRIDA

"I am at war with myself, it's true, you couldn't possibly know to what extent . . . I say contradictory things that are, we might say, in real tension; they are what construct me, make me live, and will make me die."

translated by PASCAL-ANNE BRAULT and MICHAEL NAAS

$15.95 / $17.95 CAN
978-1-61219-094-5
ebook: 978-1-61219-032-7

ROBERTO BOLAÑO: THE LAST INTERVIEW

"Posthumous: It sounds like the name of a Roman gladiator, an unconquered gladiator. At least that's what poor Posthumous would like to believe. It gives him courage."

translated by SYBIL PEREZ and others

$15.95 / $17.95 CAN
978-1-61219-095-2
ebook: 978-1-61219-033-4

THE LAST INTERVIEW SERIES

DAVID FOSTER WALLACE: THE LAST INTERVIEW

"I don't know what you're thinking or what it's like inside you and you don't know what it's like inside me. In fiction . . . we can leap over that wall itself in a certain way."

$15.95 / $15.95 CAN
978-1-61219-206-2
ebook: 978-1-61219-207-9

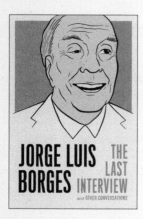

JORGE LUIS BORGES: THE LAST INTERVIEW

"Believe me: the benefits of blindness have been greatly exaggerated. If I could see, I would never leave the house, I'd stay indoors reading the many books that surround me."

translated by KIT MAUDE
edited by GLORIA LOPEZ LECUBE

$15.95 / $15.95 CAN
978-1-61219-204-8
ebook: 978-1-61219-205-5